SUCCESS WITH
SHARPENING

SUCCESS WITH
SHARPENING

RALPH LAUGHTON

GUILD OF MASTER CRAFTSMAN PUBLICATIONS LTD

First published 2004 by
Guild of Master Craftsman Publications Ltd,
166 High Street, Lewes,
East Sussex BN7 1XU

ISBN 1 86108 329 7
A catalogue record of this book is available from the
British Library.

Publisher: Paul Richardson
Art Director: Ian Smith
Production Manager: Hilary MacCallum
Managing Editor: Gerrie Purcell
Editor: James Evans

Cover design: Gilda Pacitti
Book design: Ian Hunt
Typeface: Palatino and Frutiger

Colour origination: CTT Reproduction, London
Printed and bound: Stamford Press, Singapore

Acknowledgements

I would like to thank the following people for their help in the compilation of this book.

First, I would like to thank Roy Child of Peter Child Woodturning Supplies for his help in compiling the information on sharpening turning tools and the use of grinding wheels. His years of experience proved invaluable and informative. Thanks are also extended to my good friends Mark Cass (Editor, *New Woodworking*) and Stuart Lawson (Editor, *The Router*) for their help, support and understanding while working on this book at the same time as writing regularly for their respective magazines. But most of all to my long-suffering wife, Sue, who has not only read each and every word, but has fed and watered a sometimes grumpy and tired husband without complaint.

Thanks are also due to the good people at Axminster Power Tool Centre for the supply of products and photographs, to Henry Taylor Tools for the supply of carving tools and to BriMarc for the supply of Veritas, Tormek and Flexcut products.

Contents

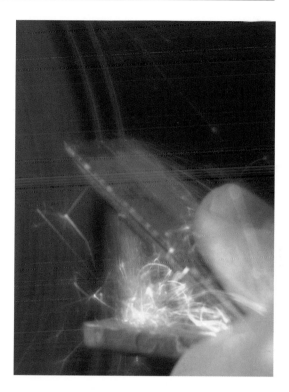

Part 2:
Machine Sharpening

Part 3:
Sharpening in Practice

Introduction

From absolute beginner to seasoned professional, everyone has his or her own method for achieving a sharp edge. This can vary from the ill informed or misguided to the 'perfect' method that has been used for years.

In truth, there are no right or wrong ways of successfully achieving a sharp edge; there are just different methods of reaching a common goal.

There are, however, lots of things that will stop you from achieving that elusive sharp edge, and sharpening is a skill that is acquired and refined over the years. For the novice, the main hurdle to climb is one of confidence.

The first thing to understand is that edged tools are supplied with the intention that the user at least undertakes the final honing. It is wrong to assume that the supplied edge is as good as it gets – in fact, this is just about as far away from the truth as you can get. This misapprehension is underlined by two statements made by friends and family: 'the chisel was blunt so I went out and bought a new one,' and 'what are you doing? I've only just bought that plane.'

It is true to say that most chisels and planes sold today will 'do the job' straight out of the box. With tools so readily available and a lack of practical education about sharpening, this is almost a prerequisite, and it is little wonder that the myth has become a reality. Manufacturers have been quick to exploit this situation,

KEY POINT

Most newly purchased tools are sharp enough to perform adequately, but it is wrong to assume that the supplied edge is the sharpest that can be achieved.

for example by marketing planes with disposable blades. These planes certainly help the budding do-it-yourself enthusiast to trim the odd door, but they are not going to hold up against a craftsman-built bench plane.

ABOVE A mirror finish after honing and polishing (left), compared to a similar chisel as it would have been supplied.

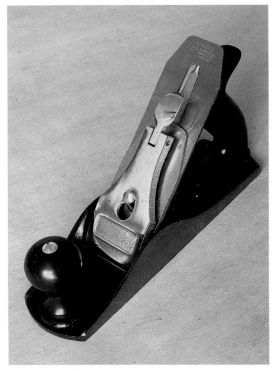

ABOVE Cheap planes are made to satisfy the DIY market, but quality is sacrificed.

ABOVE The end grain of softwood – achieving a clean cut is the ultimate test of a tool's sharpness.

How sharp is sharp?

You could say the front of a ship is sharp, or the tip of the surgeon's scalpel, but each needs to satisfy totally different criteria. The same can be said about edged tools. Some tools need slender edges designed to make light cuts, others need much stronger edges for chopping. Whatever the end use, an edge is achieved in the same manner, and therefore the processes employed to achieve that edge are similar in principle.

Materials play a big part in obtaining a sharp cutting edge. The better the quality of the materials used the better the edge that can be obtained. This has already

ⓕOCUS ON:

The Perfect Cutting Edge

A sharp edge is created when two planes converge. At the point where the convergence is such that they have no dimension, a perfect cutting edge would be formed. This is the theory, but in practice it is impossible to achieve. The edge is the finest point at which the material can still exist. As material must have a thickness, the edge is compromised. The objective when sharpening is to make that compromise as negligible as possible.

ⓕOCUS ON:

The Perfect
Cutting Edge

been determined once you are holding the tool in readiness for sharpening. It goes without saying that if the tool is cheap little time will have been spent making it and its components. This will have a direct bearing on the resultant edge. It is not possible to make a cheap tool perform as well as an expensive one just by spending hours grinding and honing the edge to the best of your ability. Having said that, you will close the gap considerably. It is amazing the amount of difference careful, frequent honing can make to even the poorest tools.

FOCUS ON:

Crucible Steel

FOCUS ON:

Crucible Steel

Clock maker Benjamin Huntsman (1704–76) spent a lot of time developing a high-carbon steel (known as 'crucible steel' after the vessel in which the various constituents were melted and mixed) in order to produce efficient clock springs. In the course of his efforts he discovered that his steel held a better edge than the contemporary steel being used by the local Sheffield cutlers. He tried to interest them in his new product, but they felt it was too hard to work. French cutlers, however, embraced the steel with open arms and bought all he could produce.

The Sheffield cutlers soon found their market being taken over by the now superior French product, and after a time started to buy Huntsman's steel. The demand for crucible steel continued to rise and in the late 1700s Huntsman moved his steel-making plant to the Don Valley. The area subsequently became home to specialized steel production.

Because of its hardness, the crucible steel was very brittle and therefore prone to breaking. In order to maintain the edge and give it some toughness, it was usually laminated with a ductile piece of wrought iron. On early planes and chisels the lamination is quite visible at the grinding bevel.

ABOVE The lamination on this plane iron can just be seen as the grinding progresses.

Today, steel technology is taken for granted. We assume that someone has used the most suitable material for whatever the use. In reality, cost and volume of sales dictates material use.

Components that were at one time lovingly crafted are the next target of outsourcing in an effort to reduce costs. The result is a product that bears a well-known brand name but is in fact an inferior substitute sacrificing quality for cost.

As the world becomes smaller due to the never-ending advance of communication and travel technology, so, in turn, the manufacturing base becomes wider. A cheap plane, for example, could be conceived (usually copied) in a design office, have its parts sourced from all corners of the earth, and be assembled

KEY POINT

ABOVE A comparison: (left to right) an old Stanley No.5, a modern Stanley No.5, and the ultimate British-made No.5, a Clifton.

in a factory where the workers may not even know what it is. The iron will be made from the cheapest steel available and have the minimum of finish.

In fairness, our demand for cheaper goods has forced the price down. These middle-of-the-range products serve a large market and make tools of reasonable quality available to the mass public. The cutting edge is usually made from a high-quality carbon cast steel. However, the quality end of the market is left to smaller specialist firms that supply traditional products at realistic prices.

Disposable tools

In an age in which we are all encouraged to recycle on the one hand, we are bombarded with labour-saving products on the other, and 'labour saving' often equates directly to 'disposable'. In addition, the cheaper the product the less respect it commands. A couple of years ago, I was visiting a member of my family. He was re-hanging a door so that it would open in the opposite direction. He said that it had taken longer than expected because he had to go and buy a new chisel. He went on to explain that the old one he had owned for several years was now blunt. The idea that he might be able to re-sharpen his old chisel seemed remote (nor had he thought that it might be possible to improve on the factory grind).

There are some areas where a disposable edge makes a lot of sense. The surgeon's scalpel is an obvious candidate as there are other considerations to take into account, such as hygiene. In the workshop we all use disposable bladed knives like the ubiquitous 'Stanley' knife, now used as a generic term for any make of utility knife. Although it is perfectly possible to re-sharpen these blades, more often than not it is easier just to replace it with a new one.

I have been known to sharpen the odd Stanley knife blade in an emergency (i.e. when I've run out of new ones), but this is not really practical. The edge is so hard that it tends to chip and notch rather than just lose its edge, and getting it back to a good straight edge can take some time. The other thing to take into account is the tool's intended use. How good does the edge need to be? A utility knife is not a fine finishing tool like a plane or chisel.

KEY POINT

KEY POINT

Not all woodworking tools should be seen as disposable; throwing away an old chisel or plane iron because the cutting edge is dull is highly wasteful.

One product that would have completely bemused the craftsmen of old is the disposable plane blade. My uncle was an old-school carpenter and cabinetmaker. He also regarded plane irons and chisels as disposable, the only difference is the time scale. The plane he had as a boy had a disposable iron in it – according to him, his grandchildren would probably need to replace it after it had been ground and honed away after years of sharpening. Throwing a blade away just because it was dull would have been seen as wasteful at the very least.

One particular problem is the skill level of those who buy tools, especially since the arrival of the DIY craze in the 1950s. Not only that but the man in the street had money to spend, and the start of the marketing age was here. The trouble was that teaching DIY enthusiasts to sharpen chisels was not good business for manufacturers who were looking to expand their market. Far better to throw it away and buy a new one. Fifty years on and the story has compounded itself with masses of products to choose from and very little in the way of education at the point of sale.

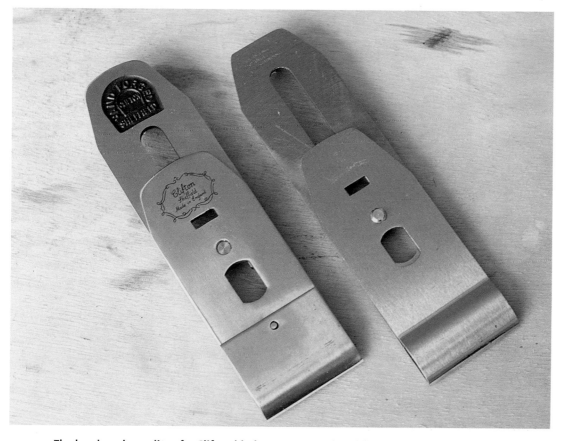

ABOVE The hand-made quality of a Clifton blade, or mass-produced functionality – take your pick.

Sharpening: an overview

It doesn't matter how much care you take or how much effort you put in to improving your woodworking, if the tools that you are using are not sharp, the job will become a chore and your work will suffer. Sharp tools are the number-one, must-have accessory for the successful woodworker. Trying to force a blunt edge into a piece of wood requires more power and results in less control. So before you can learn how to use your tools, you must learn how to sharpen them properly.

Anyone can put an edge on a tool. There is no magic involved; it is not akin to one of the arts. Nor do you have to be born with a talent or come from a long line of sharpening experts. You don't even need to be wealthy in order to invest in the best sharpening stones or machines. All you need is an understanding of the process and the time to practice – lots of practice.

Although plenty of books and videos have been written on the subject of sharpening, most of them champion a particular method or two. The truth is that most of us have a preferred method that we use. I suspect that if I had been confined to a workshop building furniture I too would have found a route that suited me and stuck to it. The quest for new methods has

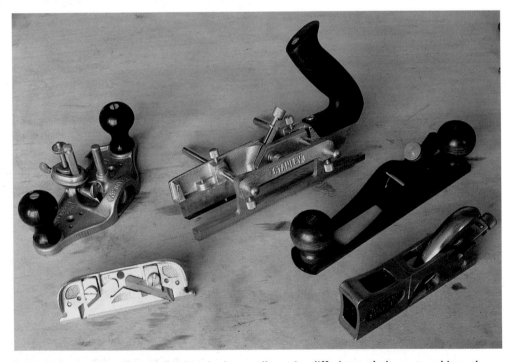

ABOVE A selection of specialist bench planes. All require differing techniques to achieve the same goal: a sharp cutting edge

always interested me, and writing about my passion has enabled me to experiment with methods that I would not otherwise have found time for. What follows in this book is an overview of the different methods and products that will help you to get close to the impossible dream – an edge with no dimension.

I will show you several methods of sharpening the same types of tool in part three (see page 91), although in reality you will find a method that suits you and that will be your mainstay. For years I used the same method of sharpening; it was only when a new technique came to my attention a few years ago that I started to use something different on a regular basis. I changed because the technology had evolved and the abrasive had become more sophisticated. The edge produced was as good as before (or perhaps even a bit better), but the real reason for change was that the process itself had become quicker. As a result, I am able to spend more time woodworking and less time sharpening tools.

For most of us, the structure of the material is something we have to 'buy in'; once the tool is in our hands there is little we can do to change its properties, other than detrimentally. However, simply refining the standard of finish to the edge can make a huge difference, whatever material is used.

FOCUS ON:

Heat Treatment

The better the quality of material used and the care put in to producing it, the better the edge it is possible to obtain. The edge will be hardened and tempered to a specific temperature to give it optimum performance for the intended task. The aim of the heat-treating is to change the structure of the metal to produce a tough edge that will not dull too quickly, yet not be so hard that it becomes brittle. For this reason it is important to keep the edge cool during sharpening. Excess heat can draw the temper, rendering the edge softer than intended. This will severely reduce the effectiveness of the edge and, consequently, the working life of the tool. (For more, see page 65.)

FOCUS ON:

Heat Treatment

The first thing to consider is that an edge is made by the convergence of two surfaces: the back and the bevel. To produce a good finish, both of these need to be as smooth as possible.

Smoothing the back

Let us consider a run-of-the-mill tool shop chisel: the sort of tool that most of us have and use. The blade will have a machine-ground finish to the back and the bevel. If this were to be magnified, the surface would resemble a ploughed field.

However, smoothing the surface of the bevel would only solve half the problem. The surface at the point of intersection between the grinding bevel and the back would be broken up into a serrated edge by the grinding marks, and the resultant edge would still be substandard. To avoid this, the back of the blade first needs to be smoothed and flattened.

Smoothing the bevel

After the back has been flattened, it is time to establish the bevel. It is a myth that you must be able to achieve this without any help in order to consider yourself competent, especially if you are trying to adjust an incorrect primary grinding. Each tool requires a slightly different technique, and these will be covered in part three (see page 91).

The final cutting angle is usually added as a secondary or 'micro' bevel. There are several reasons expressed for doing this, some relate to heat build-up, others express the advantages of mechanical strength. My own reason is purely one of convenience: it is much quicker to hone a new secondary bevel than it is to hone the entire primary bevel every time the edge becomes dull or acquires a light nick.

This sequence outlines the sharpening process in its most basic form and will be repeated (with variations) for most edged tools: flattening the back (ABOVE), honing the primary bevel (OPPOSITE, TOP) and then the secondary bevel (OPPOSITE, BOTTOM).

Part 1:
Sharpening by Hand

1:1 Sharpening methods: old and new

My first encounter with the art of sharpening was a large lump of natural stone that my grandfather used for sharpening his kitchen knives. Even allowing for the distortions of childhood memories, it was a big lump of stone – it must have been 20in (500mm) long and about 3x4in (75x100mm) in cross section.

That lump of stone was personal to him; the constant sharpening action of one man over a period of years had shaped it to a deep curve and it was understood that nobody else used it.

However, this traditional view of sharpening is a far cry from today's multinational industry and the vast range of products and techniques it makes available.

ABOVE Modern manmade bench stones and slip stones. The selection available is enormous and this is but a small selection of oil- and waterstones.

My uncle's planes and chisels were generally sharpened on a trusty oilstone, courtesy of the Carborundum Company. In the hands of this craftsman, the effortless 'lick' of the stone gave a false impression of simplicity – this was a skill brought about through years of experience and hard work in getting the tool as he wanted it. Here was a man who could chat about a day out to the woods and, using touch alone, simultaneously hone a perfect bevel at whatever angle he desired with no effort at all. Now, forty years on, we have turned a mundane task that became second nature into a huge industry. What is more, I find myself adding to it in an effort to get some simplicity back into what should be an uncomplicated subject.

KEY POINT

'Carborundum' is the trade name for a type of silicone-carbide bench stone, also known (more generically) as an oilstone, which is used for hand sharpening as well as other types of grinding.

Most of us, me included, have preferred working methods and favourite abrasives that we like to use. Today, more than ever, the choice has broadened to encompass not only modern manufacturing technology, but also different working methods and products from around the globe. All of these have their merits and should be investigated even if, like me, you have your own routine. Writing this book has introduced me to methods I knew about but had not used, and I found that a mix of disciplines could be used to give me the edge I wanted. Although this book will cover most of the available options, I am not going to advocate one method over another; the 'right' one will depend on the precise nature of the job in hand.

Working the edge by hand can be a rewarding task, and although you shouldn't expect to get it right the first time, it is not as hard as it might seem. There is no magic shortcut I can give that will enable you to be able to hand grind and hone instantly; it is a skill that improves with practice. Traditional oilstones are just the start. Sharpening by hand can be carried out on any abrasive surface that will cut the metal. This can be as coarse as 60-grit silicon-carbide paper, at one end of the scale, or as fine as the nap of newsprint. These are obviously extremes, but somewhere between the two is just the right degree of coarseness to suit your needs.

ABOVE Honing and stropping surfaces: MDF, leather, extra-fine wet-and-dry paper and even newspaper.

1:2 Oilstones and waterstones

Most of us must have come into contact with the ubiquitous oilstone. Unless it belonged to a tradesman, this stone was generally either pristine (and still in its wrapper) or well used and covered in oil and sawdust – perhaps a victim of the newly developing DIY culture of the 1950s.

If you have such a stone and intend to put it to work, check to see if it is serviceable first. If it is new and unused there probably won't be a problem. The box or even the stone itself will identify exactly what it is and whether it is natural or manmade. The sticky, sawdust-covered variety may be another matter. The chances are that it is a medium-grit carborundum stone. Whether or not it can be salvaged will depend on how badly it has been abused and just what the sticky stuff is. Simply scraping off the worst of the rubbish and rinsing the stone in mineral spirits or turpentine can make a huge difference.

Unless an old stone has sentimental significance, it is probably not worth dealing with. If it does, it is best put to one side and dealt with after some experience with known materials has been gained. The cost of a new oilstone is not high, and at least you will be starting with something that has realistic and qualified limitations.

TECHNIQUE:

Preparing an
Oilstone

TECHNIQUE:

Preparing an Oilstone

Before being put to use an oilstone needs to be charged with oil. To do this, soak the stone in honing oil until it has reached saturation point (the time this will take will vary depending on the porosity of the stone). Once it has 'filled' with oil, wipe off any excess and set it in a wooden box. It is a good idea to charge the wood of the box with the same oil, as a dry box may absorb some oil from the stone.

Each time the stone is used, more oil will be added to the surface to act as a lubricant. If the stone has not been properly charged beforehand, the new oil will simply seep into the stone, causing the surface to clog with metal filings and glaze over. If this happens, the stone can usually be cleaned off with a soak in paraffin, before being recharged with oil.

ABOVE A new oilstone, and its box, primed with oil and ready for use.

(FOCUS ON:

Natural and Manmade Stone

Bench stones were initially cut from natural stone, and usually bore the name of their place of origin, such as Turkey stone and Arkansas stone. In the early days of abrasive stones, natural stones were still an important option, as the manufactured versions could not achieve such a fine grain. However, although stone is still quarried and used for sharpening, the majority of stones in use today are manmade. The purest examples of natural stones are becoming harder and harder to find. Indeed, some of the more sought-after examples of natural stone can change hands for large sums, especially some of the natural Japanese waterstones. But who is going to sharpen a chisel on a valuable natural stone, knowing that using it will make it virtually worthless?

Luckily, companies like Norton of America saw the need for synthetic abrasives and set up a plant to manufacture the world's first manmade precision grinding wheels in 1885. Many companies now distribute a vast range of abrasive products around the world, and it is possible to purchase a wide range of compounds, grits and hardnesses of stone.

Today, manmade stones offer many advantages for day-to-day use by the craftsman. As technology has improved, so have synthetic stones. Finer and finer methods of suspension and better distribution of the grit throughout the stone have been achieved, giving a guaranteed uniformity to the cutting rate. The exact rate of wear can also be determined by making the resin bond harder or softer. However, the greatest advantage today is price: cheap synthetic stones cost very little and, providing you understand their limitations, can be good value for money.

ABOVE A selection of old oilstones: manmade and natural.

(FOCUS ON:

Natural and Manmade Stone

Using bench stones

Bench stones are intended for sharpening straight-edged tools such as chisels and plane irons. To this end, keeping a bench stone flat is of paramount importance for producing a good cutting edge. The sharpening action used can help achieve

this, and you should aim to use as much of the stone as possible. This is especially important when sharpening narrow tools like delicate woodcarving chisels. Moving the tool in a figure of eight pattern over the face of the stone is one method. Alternatively, use straight strokes up and down along the length of the stone and then across the diagonals. Wider tools, such as bench-plane irons, can be run straight up and down the stone's length.

(KEY POINT

(KEY POINT

To get a flat, straight cutting edge, the abrasive must also be flat. Use a bench stone's entire surface as you hone, keeping the pressure and grinding angle constant, to prevent it from becoming uneven.

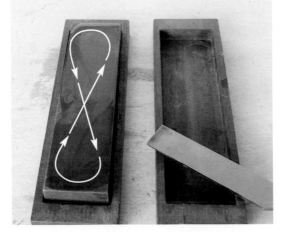

The surface of a bench stone must be kept flat if it is to produce a good, straight cutting edge. Even out the wear on a stone by adopting a figure of eight pattern of sharpening (ABOVE). Alternatively, sharpen up and down and then across the diagonals (RIGHT).

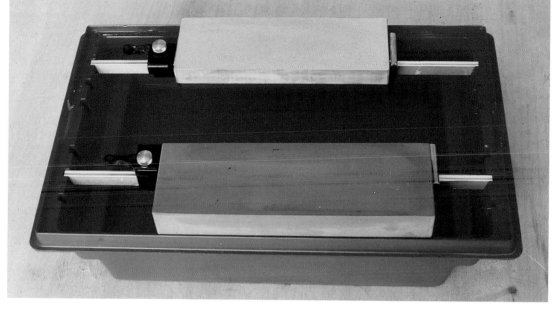

ABOVE To contain the mess created during the sharpening process, waterstones are best used over a pond. Alternatively (RIGHT), they can be held in a rubber stone clamp.

Stones maintain their abrasive surface by eroding away as sharpening takes place, revealing new, sharp grit. Eventually, even when using oilstones or waterstones with great care, it may be necessary to re-face them in order to regain a perfectly flat surface. This is not as daunting as it may sound. The simplest method is to rub it against another stone. If you have one, a diamond stone is ideal for this. Whatever you use, do not contaminate a stone with the wrong lubricant – i.e. never flatten a waterstone with an oilstone.

Waterstones are best used over a bath of water (known as a 'pond') and on a non-porous surface. Commercial stone ponds are available, or you can make your own. If a pond is not available or practical to use, the waterstone can be held in a stone clamp and placed on a shallow tray in an effort to contain the copious amount of water that will invariably run off of the stone. A piece of non-slip matting (like the type used to stop loose rugs sliding away on a polished floor) placed between the tray and the worktop will prevent it from sliding around during the sharpening process.

Storing bench stones

Oilstones are traditionally stored in wooden boxes. These become soaked in oil and should not be allowed to come into contact with any timber that will be used for a project – an oily patch on the surface of a finished piece will be hard, if not impossible, to disguise. In fact, to ensure that your work is not damaged, it is wise to have a dedicated sharpening area. This is just as important when using waterstones, although a drop of water on the surface of a project is not nearly as harmful as oil. The amount of mess generated when using a waterstone is considerable – they are the messiest of all sharpening mediums.

Medium and coarse waterstones should be stored in water, but fine-grained waterstones should be allowed to dry out between uses. Most importantly, store them in a frost-free environment. Water expands as it freezes, and allowing this to happen to the water trapped inside a stone can cause it to break.

KEY POINT

KEY POINT

Do not allow your waterstone or the water in which it is stored to freeze: the water will expand as it freezes and, as a result, the stone may crack.

TECHNIQUE:

Flattening a Bench Stone

Although one stone can be flattened using another, employing this method runs the risk of mixing the wrong lubricants – for example, contaminating a waterstone with oil from an oilstone.

An alternative solution is to flatten the stone on a sheet of silicon-carbide paper (also known as wet-and-dry) of around 120 grit. The silicon-carbide paper should be spray mounted to a sheet of glass or similar flat surface (a machined table is a good choice for this). Do not be tempted to use double-sided tape to secure the paper – the tape will form a ridge in the paper's surface, making it impossible to obtain a truly flat finish.

Once the flattening process has been completed, the stone(s) should be washed thoroughly. To do this, use water for waterstones, paraffin or mineral spirits for oilstones. After washing, oilstones should be recharged with honing oil by letting them soak for 10–15 minutes, and then wiped clean with a lint-free rag.

Various techniques for flattening a bench stone: with another stone (TOP), with silicon-carbide paper adhered to a flat surface (MIDDLE), and using abrasive powder and a sheet of glass (BOTTOM), a process known as 'lapping'.

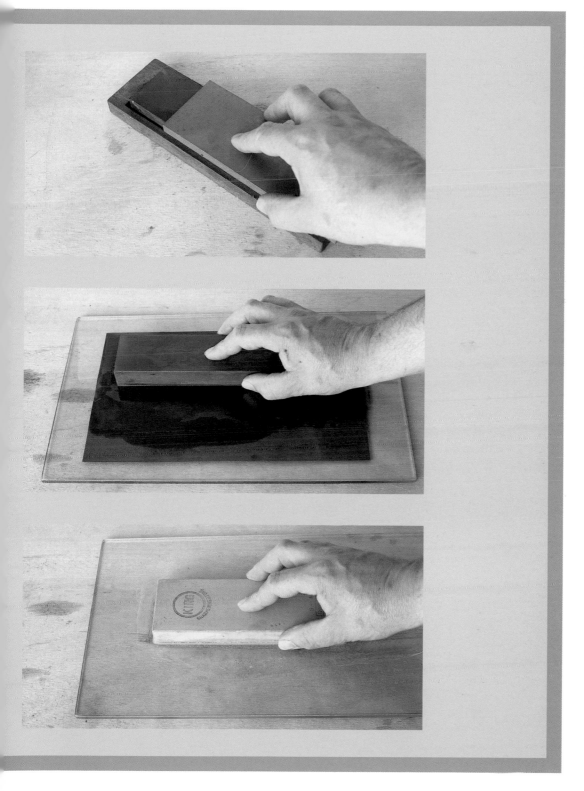

Flattening a Bench
Stone

1:3 Modern sharpening surfaces

Technology moves on, and although waterstones can now be produced with extremely fine grits, they have two disadvantages: they are messy to use, and they wear relatively quickly. So, what alternatives are available to the twenty first-century craftsperson?

Diamond stones offer fast-cutting qualities combined with stable flat surfaces that wear very slowly in use and can be used dry. Alternatively, they can be used with honing oil, water or mineral spirits as a lubricant.

Ceramic stones seem almost too good to be true, needing no lubricant and having a negligible wear rate. Not only that, they are even dishwasher safe! The advances in abrasive-paper technology have given the budding sharpener yet another viable choice.

Ceramic stones

These stones are used dry and will cut the hardest of metals. A medium-grit ceramic stone will wear only lightly with use, while fine and ultra-fine stones are so hard that

ABOVE Ceramic stones like these are the new low-maintenance, no-mess solution to bench sharpening.

they will stay flat and show little or no sign of wear over time. Maintenance could not be easier: they do not need flattening, and to clean them you can just put them in the dishwasher! Failing that, a once-over with domestic abrasive powder (e.g. Ajax) and a nylon scourer will bring a ceramic stone back to pristine condition.

As no lubricants are necessary, the sharpening process is almost clean; apart from the small amount of abraded metal, there is no mess at all. These stones are usually supplied in a plastic box and can be used on any surface. Some boxes have small non-slip pads in each corner to prevent the box from moving around during the sharpening process. In the absence of any such built-in pads, a non-slip mat will also keep the box still.

ABOVE Ceramic stones are even dishwasher proof so that they can be cleaned with a minimum of effort – how modern is that!

Diamond stones

Unlike the former examples of bench stones, diamond stones don't wear away to leave an uneven surface. The cutting surface is a thin veneer of industrial diamond bonded to a flat substrate. The cutting action is very fast, making the coarser grits ideal for initial flattening and grinding. They can also be used to maintain the flatness of other types of bench stone.

Lubrication can be by water or mineral spirits. Some stones have their abrasive bonded to a ferrous substrate, and although water can be used with them it is better to use a mineral spirits, as this will significantly reduce any risk of the stone's substrate oxidising and forming rust.

Diamond stones can be mounted in rubber-jawed bench-stone clamps or simply laid directly onto a non-slip mat. Although a lubricant is used, they do not generate anywhere near the mess of oil- or waterstones because they do not need to erode in order to reveal fresh cutting grits. An additional benefit is that loose diamond grits can be used to change the characteristics of the stone. These are mixed with some of the lubricant to form an abrasive slurry. After use, all traces of the loose abrasive must be removed from the stone and the tool in order to eliminate any risk of contamination.

ABOVE A range of the latest diamond stones and hones. As well as being an excellent option for sharpening tools, diamond stones can be used to flatten conventional oil- and waterstones.

(FOCUS ON:

Portable
Sharpening Aids

(FOCUS ON:

Portable Sharpening Aids

There are many benefits to the small 'portable' sharpening aids now available. Most importantly, a wafer-thin diamond sharpening stone, the size of a credit card, will fit in a wallet or hang on a keyring and allow you to maintain an edge wherever you are. The convenience of these small pieces of flat or shaped abrasive means that more than ever the little-and-often rule can be applied to your sharpening. How many of us can honestly say that they would stop working and find all the sharpening paraphernalia to give a dull chisel a few licks if they were kneeling at a door cutting a lock-plate recess? However, a diamond card tucked into a wallet or tool roll is going to get used.

LEFT Credit card-sized diamond sharpening. These can be carried with you anywhere, so there's no excuse for letting an edge become dull.

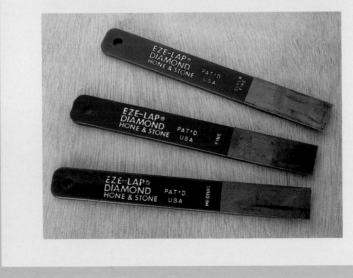

LEFT Three grades of diamond on plastic handles – ideal for on-the-job honing.

TECHNIQUE:

Lapping

TECHNIQUE:

Lapping

Using loose grits and pastes it is possible to sharpen tools on a flat surface, such as a piece of hardened steel or a sheet of glass. In fact, it is possible to use just about any stable surface that can be maintained flat; even a block of close-grained hardwood, such as maple, planed to a perfectly flat surface can be held in a vice and charged with compound. The grit can be any form of abrasive that will cut the metal of the blade.

This can be carborundum- or diamond-based purpose-made lapping grits, household products like chrome cleaner, or metal polishes. Whatever is used the method of working is the same. The lapping surface is coated with a mixture of dry grit and a lubricating medium. The tool is then worked using different levels of grit – starting with coarse and working down to fine – until the desired finish is achieved.

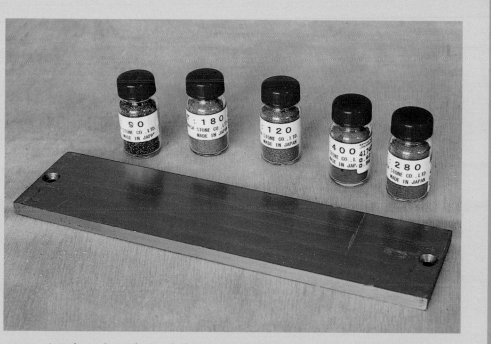

ABOVE Lapping grits and a steel plate produced in Japan and exported worldwide.

Abrasive Paper

Not so long ago, sandpaper and glasspaper were exactly that – small grains of abrasive stuck to sheets of thick paper. They were prone to clogging and the grit was easily dislodged during use.

Modern abrasive papers are a different matter altogether. The development of sophisticated adhesives and improvements in modern mass-manufacturing techniques has resulted in products that are more than capable of cutting the metal from which edged tools are made.

The choice of abrasives is enormous, but from the sharpening point of view the most significant advance is the fineness of grain. Some of the finer waterproof silicon-carbide papers, primarily intended for use in the finishing and refinishing of coachwork, are so fine that the printing on the back finds a new significance – it lets you know which side the back actually is!

When you are using a bench stone to sharpen straight-edged tools, the 'straightness' of the edge is maintained by the stone's structure. If the stone itself is flat, and providing the tool is presented

ABOVE A selection of abrasive papers.

'Wet-and-dry' is a type of fine abrasive paper that can be used with lubrication, either water or mineral spirits. The grit is of silicon carbide and the paper and glue are both waterproof.

to the stone properly, the edge will also be flat and straight. As the stone wears the profile of the edge being sharpened will mimic the surface of the abrasive. Diamond stones do not suffer from this erosion problem because their abrasive is applied to a flat reference surface instead of being an integral part of it (as is the case with conventional stones).

Similarly, the quality of the sharpened edge will be determined, in part, by the flatness of the surface a sheet of abrasive paper is applied to. The flat surface of a machine table would make a suitable surface, and a floor-standing bandsaw table is set at a comfortable height for sharpening. Plate glass is also a good material to use. This can be obtained

from glass merchants, although it is a good idea to have the edges polished. The glass needs to be fairly thick, at least ¼in (6mm). Several pieces of glass can be used, each with different grades of paper attached. A piece of MDF clamped to the bench, with a small cross-section bead applied, can be used to hold the sheet of glass.

TECHNIQUE:

Using Abrasive Paper

To use abrasive paper for sharpening, it must be secured to a flat surface using a spray adhesive. The bond this produces will not be permanent, enabling spent paper to be removed and (after the surface has been scraped clean with a bladed window scraper to ensure a smooth finish) replaced. Various grades of abrasive can be used when sharpening.

You should aim to progress through the grits, starting with a coarse grit for flattening new tools and profile grinding, and working through to the finest papers for final polishing. Make sure that the tools are wiped clean between each change of grit to avoid contamination.

KEY POINT

TECHNIQUE:

Using Abrasive Paper

41

Sharpening with abrasive paper

ABOVE A sheet of abrasive paper being used to flatten the back of a plane iron.

ABOVE High areas are abraded first.

ABOVE Once the material is being abraded evenly, the back is flat.

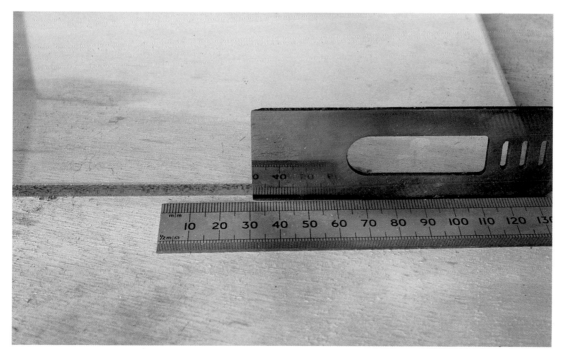

ABOVE After polishing on a finer sheet of abrasive paper, the back should be perfectly flat and show an undistorted reflection in the mirror finish.

1:4 Holding the tool

An experienced craftsman can make sharpening look like light work; a few passes of a chisel over a stone and like magic it is sharp enough to shave with.

What is missing from this picture is the years of practice, not to mention a familiarity with tools. Our craftsman is simply touching up the edge; all the hard work was done long ago.

Whether or not he used a guide to produce that original edge, there is one thing he has learnt through the passage of time and that is to keep a tool in peak condition. That means touching it up while it is still sharp, not waiting until it is dull.

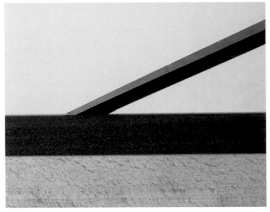

ABOVE When learning to hone by hand, start with a wide-edged blade on a bench stone. This will provide greater stability and make it easier to develop the 'feel'.

Once the initial factory grinding is done on, for example, a chisel, it is possible to feel the bevel by rocking the tool back and forth on the surface of the stone. When sharpening by hand, this position is maintained by moving the tool along the stone using the elbows and shoulders, while keeping the wrists locked parallel to the surface. Using this method, the primary bevel can be refined and subsequently honed to the desired finish. Raising the tool slightly will create a steeper angle of sharpening, and by using the same method to propel the tool across the stone it will be possible to hone a secondary bevel.

These three shots of a chisel on a bench stone show how important it is to get the honing angle right: too low (**TOP**), the correct position (**MIDDLE**), and too high (**BOTTOM**).

FOCUS ON:

Lubricants

The main purpose of using a lubricant during honing is to help prevent the surface of the stone from becoming clogged (or 'glazed'). There are two potential sources of clogging, both of which are flushed away by the lubricant. One is steel removed from the blade, and the second is crushed abrasive particles from the stone itself.

Various liquids are available, although waterstones should only ever be used with water (water is also the best lubricant to use with resin-bonded stones). There is more scope when it comes to honing oils. Any oil used needs to be free-flowing enough to lubricate the surface without masking the abrasive action, but thick enough to prevent it from running straight off the stone. Honing oil that is doing its job properly should stay mainly on the stone's surface and contain suspended particles of the waste material.

ABOVE A selection of lubricants. The plant spray bottle is a convenient dispenser for water.

A step-by-step guide on how to hone an edge by hand can be found in part three (see page 93), which also covers techniques for sharpening specific tools.

FOCUS ON:

Lubricants

KEY POINT

It is worth taking the time to acquire the skills needed to hold the tool and sharpen by hand. As well as being the fastest option, not all blades can be accommodated by honing guides, so these will need to be worked without mechanical aid.

KEY POINT

1:5 Honing guides

Presenting the tool to the stone by hand may have all the kudos of 'being an expert', but it can be one of those procedures that is more show than go.

There is no shame in using jigs – they are there to make life easier. I use honing guides most of the time, especially when grinding the primary bevel of a new tool.

Touching up the secondary bevel as the job is progressing is another matter. Two or three passes over a fine stone are all that is required, and this is easily done by hand.

In essence, all honing guides perform the same task: they hold the edge of the tool at a predetermined angle to the sharpening surface. A roller or a pair of wheels supports the guide, and, depending on its design, these can either run along the stone itself or along the work surface. Most commercial guides are of the former type and run directly on the sharpening surface. This means that the rollers and bearings will collect a fair amount of debris during use and should be thoroughly cleaned, checked and lubricated after each session. Even guides that have been used without lubricant (on ceramic stones, for example) will still need cleaning after use. This is because particles of metal and dust from the abrasive can become trapped in the bearings of the rolling device and threads of the clamping system.

ABOVE Honing guides vary in look, but all perform the same function.

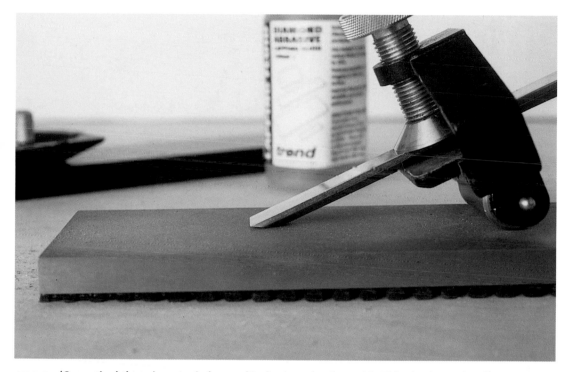

ABOVE 'Correcting' the primary grind on a chisel using a honing guide. This simple version features a clamping system to hold the tool in place and has small wheels that run directly on the sharpening surface. The guide must be cleaned after use to keep it in good working order and to prevent cross-contamination of lubricants.

KEY POINT

Several types of honing guide are available, distinguished by different styles of clamp and running gear. Essentially they all do the same thing: maintain the tool at the correct angle to the abrasive.

The other type of guide, where the roller or wheels run on a flat surface in front of or behind the stone, eliminate the worry of contamination, but have two other factors to consider. Firstly, the running surface has to be maintained to the same standard as the face of the stone. Secondly, the build has to be far more substantial to avoid any flexing within the, necessarily, much longer frame of the guide.

Guides also have different types of grip to hold the tool in place. Those that grip the edges of the blade can only sharpen straight-bladed tools that have edges square to their sides, such as conventional plane irons and bench chisels. Guides that have a clamping screw arrangement can also be used for holding skew-edged tools.

KEY POINT

TECHNIQUE:

Cleaning Honing
Guides

TECHNIQUE:

Cleaning Honing Guides

A honing guide collects a lot of waste matter during the sharpening process and must be cleaned thoroughly after use. First, rinse off any debris using mineral spirits or water (depending on the honing lubricant used during sharpening). Once clean, lightly lubricate the moving parts and remove any excess oil. This needs to be done with great care if the jig is to be used on a sharpening surface that does not use an oil-based lubricant; a waterstone, for example, will be permanently damaged if it is contaminated with oil. Remove as much of the surplus oil as you can with a lint-free cloth, then lay a sheet of kitchen paper on a flat surface and run the guide along it a couple of times in both directions (you should also do this before using the jig again). The jig can then be stored ready for next time.

Cleaning the guides after use is vital to ensure that any loose abrasive grit is removed from the workings. Mineral spirits is used to clean a jig that has been used on an oilstone (ABOVE), while water is used on jigs that have been used on waterstones (TOP RIGHT). All moving parts need lubricating (RIGHT) and any excess oil should be wiped off.

Selecting and using a honing guide

Although it is possible to make your own, it is easier to use one of the vast range of commercial guides currently available. The main difference between the various models is the way in which they hold the tool and the size and shape of the transport device (roller, wheels or ball bearing). They all have their uses, but no single guide will accommodate all tools. If you only use bench chisels and planes, most honing guides will accommodate your needs. However, a different gauge will be required when a small specialist plane blade or a skew-edged chisel needs to be honed.

Whichever version you employ, the object is to clamp the tool at a set position. This needs to be measured accurately, and lots of honing guides have the relevant information stamped or cast into them. It is imperative that a conventional square-edged tool is held in the clamping device so that it is presented square to the sharpening surface. With jigs such as the Eclipse 36, the blade is held square by the action of the jaws. The distance from

FOCUS ON:

The Eclipse Guide

One of the most common honing guides available is the small, usually grey, compact jig made by Eclipse (but sold under several brand names). This little guide is robust and it is easy to set the right angle. The jaws open wide enough to hold most chisels or plane irons, and the method of clamping ensures that the blade is held square to the stone for honing. This does mean that it cannot be used for honing skew-edged tools, and guides that secure the tool from above are required for these tools.

ABOVE The ubiquitous Eclipse 36 honing guide has many imitators.

FOCUS ON:

The Eclipse Guide

53

ABOVE This Stanley guide has a built-in measure to set the tool at the correct projection.

the tool edge to the casting of the guide can be set easily with the aid of a combination square or a depth gauge.

Some types of guide allow for varying amounts of sideways adjustment. Although this is useful for honing skew-edged tools, it adds another factor to the setting of the guide. Some guides have alignment marks on them to aid the setting up, but it is still advisable to check that the setting of the tool is square before you commence any honing.

An alternative to measuring the amount that the tool protrudes from the guide is to measure the angle of the tool in respect to the sharpening surface. This angle must

ABOVE No longer available but well worth hunting out second hand is the Record 'Edge Tool Honer'. The ball-bearing runner allows for sideways movement, which lets you hone skew chisels and some very small plane blades like the side rebate blade shown here. The coin is just used to even out the pressure exerted by the clamp.

always be measured perpendicular to the cutting edge, and is best achieved using a template or jig. Veritas make a jig of this type as part of their 'sharpening system', which consists of an angle-setting jig and a roller clamp that is attached to the tool.

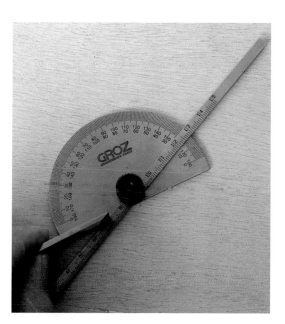

RIGHT Using a protractor to measure a 25° bevel on a general-purpose chisel.

TECHNIQUE:

Setting the Edge Angle

TECHNIQUE:

Setting the Edge Angle

To achieve a specific edge angle, a tool needs to be positioned accurately in the honing guide. A number of items are available to aid this, and these can also be used to measure an existing edge angle. As well as commercially available products, simple templates can be made and mounted in the sharpening area of your workshop. Square stops can be made to set tools at particular lengths, which can be a real timesaver when trying to set a small skew plane iron into a honing guide. A whole selection of angle templates can be cut from card or sheets of model-makers' plastic card.

ABOVE Angle-setting templates can easily be made in the workshop. Those shown here are simply cut from card.

1:6 Slips, cones and strops

So far all the abrasives discussed have been flat. That is to say, they are primarily used to sharpen flat-bladed tools like plane irons and chisels. But what about shaped cutting edges, such as those found on gouges? Although a flat abrasive can be used to sharpen the outer, convex side of a curved blade it is of no use at all on a concave face. The same applies to V-bladed tools.

Old bench stones can be given a new lease of life by reshaping them to comply with the particular tool that requires sharpening. Over the years I have acquired all manner of second-hand sharpening stones. The good ones are used for the purpose they were intended; any that have been badly abused or broken are used as 'stock' for making shaped stones for special purposes. Today, however, this practice is hardly worth the effort. Slip stones of various shapes and cone-shaped stones have always been on the market, but are now cheaper and more readily available than ever before. They can be obtained in a vast selection of profiles, grades and types.

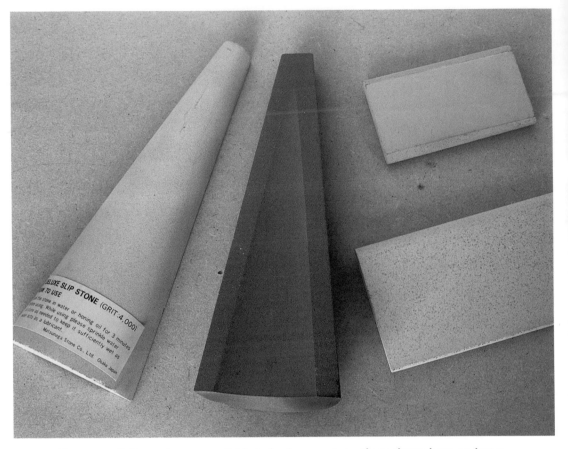

ABOVE The range of slips and cones available today is enormous – those shown here are just a selection of what is on offer. It is also possible to use old bench stones by reshaping them to fit a specific tool profile.

Teardrop-shaped slip stones are used for sharpening gouges and carving chisels. The size of slip stone is matched as closely as possible to the inner radius of the tool. The stone is drawn across the ground bevel in even strokes, taking care to sharpen the entire edge. If the tool has a convex bevel this can be sharpened on a flat stone or on the flat side of a shaped slip stone. Care must be taken to keep the tool moving across the bevel in order to prevent a flat area being generated.

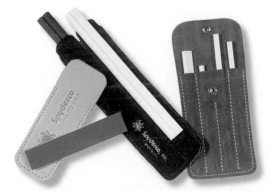

ABOVE Small ceramic slip stones come in all sorts of sizes. The edges of the leather pouches can be used to strop the inside of small gouges.

Cone-shaped slip stones have both convex and concave faces which will 'mould' themselves to your tools once you have worked them in, and can help prevent the flat areas being produced. Triangular-shaped slips will take care of the V-shaped tools, and there are round, half-round, diamond and thin flat slips available. In fact, just about every conceivable profile is now produced commercially and sold by the large tool retailers as well as small specialist suppliers.

Stropping

Stropping is the final polishing of an edge. What you are trying to achieve is a mirror finish to the edge without rounding it over. Only microscopic amounts of material are removed, and for this reason a blade must be stropped regularly to keep the edge in peak condition. If you wait until the edge is dull, you will have to strop the edge for a considerable amount of time to regain the degree of sharpness you started with.

FOCUS ON:

Carvers' Shaped Stones

Sharpening carvers' sweeps requires a concave groove to be made in the surface of a stone to match the curvature of the edge. This can be produced in the surface of a conventional bench stone, although it is now possible to purchase stones with grooves of various sizes already moulded into the surface. These will give you a start and can be worked to shape as you sharpen.

One side of a carvers' shaped stone is generally kept flat. This can be used to sharpen carving knives and other straight-edged carving tools.

When used in conjunction with a selection of slip stones, and a strop for final polishing, all your carving tools can be kept sharp and ready for use.

ABOVE Specially profiled stones and slips for carvers' gouges.

FOCUS ON:

Carvers' Shaped Stones

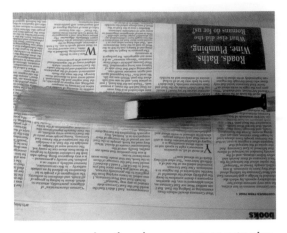

ABOVE Stropping the edge on newspaper to give a fine finish.

Strops can be made from all sorts of material. Leather immediately springs to mind because of the traditional barber's strop, but all sorts of things can be used. Wood, card and newspaper all have their place, with or without adding an abrasive compound to aid the process. The finer the abrasive, the finer the scratches it will make on the surface of the material that is being abraded.

The extent to which you pursue this practice really depends on the tool and the discipline. Generally, fine blades like those found on delicate carving chisels are more likely to be finished or retouched in this manner. Indeed, once the bevel has been established by initial grinding, some tools will be kept sharp for their entire working life by stropping. The only reason to grind the edge again would be if it has sustained some damage, or if the profile of the bevel needs to be changed.

Carving tools can be stropped on pieces of wood profiled to fit the tool, using the tool itself to produce the desired contours. A polishing compound is worked into the surface of the timber and the tool is stropped on that. Both inner and outer profiles can be stropped in this manner. Rolls of leather or leather wrapped around a length of dowel will also make for good profile strops.

KEY POINT

KEY POINT

To keep a fine cutting edge in peak condition and minimize the need for re-grinding, it should be retouched regularly using a strop made of wood or leather, and not be allowed to become dull.

ABOVE A proprietary profiled strop and block of abrasive compound.

ⓕFOCUS ON:

Burnishers

ⓕFOCUS ON:

Burnishers

Commercial burnishers consist of a smooth, hardened-steel shaft held in a handle, and come in four shapes: triangular, round, oval and teardrop. Their main use is to 'turn an edge' on a cabinet scraper. The edge of the scraper is first squared using a file or a bench stone, and a burr or 'hook' is formed using a burnisher. The scraper is then placed flat on the edge of a bench and the burnisher used to 'turn' the hook and so create a cutting edge. Almost any steel surface can be used for this, but having a tool designed for the job makes sense: a burnisher is made from hardened steel to ensure that it is harder than the scraper, and smooth so that it does not abrade the edge or remove any steel.

A sequence of shots demonstrating how to turn a 'hook' on a cabinet scraper: squaring the edge of a cabinet scraper (ABOVE), creating the burr using a burnisher (RIGHT, TOP), and finally turning the burr (RIGHT).

Part 2:
Machine Sharpening

Why overheating is a problem

Because its steel has been heat treated by the manufacturer, a plane iron or chisel will have an even temper (i.e. strength) along its entire length. As long as you prevent the steel from overheating, the edge will retain the same qualities throughout its working life, even when the blade is ground down by years of use and sharpening.

It all starts to go wrong if the friction caused during grinding overheats the metal – a particular problem with thin, delicate tools, as their low mass means that they can absorb less heat. You can see the temperature increase because the steel starts to change colour. A small amount of coloration at the tip is unavoidable, but this is not detrimental to the life of the tool. What you don't want to see is a big change, with bands of colour appearing along the tool, starting with pale yellows and moving through to deep blues as the temperature increases. By doing this you are destroying the even temper of the steel (or 'drawing the temper'), and as a consequence it will no longer hold an edge. Once this has happened, the only solution is to grind away the affected areas, although this may not be possible in severe cases and must be done without causing further overheating.

FOCUS ON:

Tempering

KEY POINT

FOCUS ON:

Tempering

The cutting edge of a blade needs certain qualities in order to maintain a good working edge. The harder it is, the longer it will stay sharp; but this has to be balanced with the fact that the harder the steel is, the more brittle it will become. A compromise between brittle/hard and malleable/soft has to be found in order to produce a blade that is hard enough to hold an edge, yet strong enough not to chip or break.

Fortunately, the properties of steel (i.e. strength, hardness, ductility, malleability and so on) can be altered through heat treatment. To obtain the correct balance, the steel used to make a tool is subjected to a finely controlled sequence of temperature changes, a process known as 'tempering'. The steel is first heated to a predetermined temperature, and then held there (or 'soaked') for a set period of time before being cooled (or 'quenched') at a specified rate.

KEY POINT

Allowing a blade to overheat while grinding will alter the properties of the steel, making it harder to maintain a cutting edge and reducing the effectiveness of the tool.

TECHNIQUE:

Controlling Heat
Build-up

TECHNIQUE:

Controlling Heat Build-up

In order to prevent the blade from overheating during grinding, the tool should only be presented to the wheel in short, deliberate advances. Withdrawing the tool frequently will allow the heat to dissipate and stop it from building up too much. Quenching the tool in water between grinds can further speed up cooling. Many proprietary grinder stands have small cups fitted for this purpose, although large turning tools or hefty mortise chisels may need a bigger reservoir to dissipate the heat faster. A steel pail (tin bucket) half full of water is ideal. This can be placed on the floor at the base of a grinder stand – just take care not to kick it over!

or damaged wheel can quite literally explode due to the forces exerted on it by centrifugal force.

I have only seen this happen once: during a metalwork class when a chisel became wedged between the stone and the guard, causing the grinder to jam and tripping the power. The teacher removed the chisel and inspected the wheel, then instructed everyone to stand back while he gave it a test run. I don't think he expected it to go, but go it did, with a sound like a gun going off – and the steel guard looked as if it had been used for target practice.

While the relatively small wheels of the light machines discussed here are not going to destruct with as much force as the old floor-standing 440v machines of my school days, I would not want to be standing in front of one that does. To ensure safety, you should always check the wheel of a machine before you power it up. Make sure there are no visible cracks or chips – and always wear eye protection.

Safety

When it comes to safety in the workshop, three things are imprinted on my brain from my school days: never walk around with an unguarded blade, never leave the chuck key in a lathe or drill press, and never stand in front of a high-speed grinder when you hit the start button.

If the first two are obvious, the third may seem less so. However, not enough is said to outline this danger, and it is important to be aware that an out-of-balance

KEY POINT

Even light grinding wheels can shatter dangerously. For safety, you should always check the wheel for defects before use, wear eye protection, and stand to one side when starting the grinder up.

KEY POINT

2:2 Powered grinders

Loosely speaking, the term 'sharpening' can be divided into three separate processes: grinding (i.e. removing metal to establish or modify the primary bevel), honing (i.e. refining the edge) and stropping (i.e. polishing the edge).

If I were writing this book fifty years ago, this section would, in the main, be about grinding – machines did the grinding, stones the honing, and a leather strop was used for the final polishing. If you needed to grind a bevel at home it was either done on a hand or foot-driven grinding wheel, or you faced a long slog on the coarsest bench stone in your possession.

However, recent developments in grinders and abrasive wheels have made a vast difference to machine sharpening, and powered grinders can now also be used to hone an edge to a fine finish.

Dry grinders

In principle, a grinder is a very simple machine. The standard layout is a motor, enclosed in a housing, with a shaft protruding at each end to hold the abrasive wheels. Other than an on/off switch, guards and tool rests, that is about it. Basic machines can be obtained fairly cheaply, and these tend to have rather coarse, grey corundum grinding wheels (for more on grinding wheels, see page 77). These are fine for general-purpose use, by which I mean general grinding, but are not the most delicate cutting medium. With care the rough shape of the bevel can be

Use the right equipment for the job in hand: a high-speed grinder fitted with a coarse grinding wheel will generate too much heat for sharpening delicate tools. Consider fitting softer wheels or using a half-speed grinder.

created, but the process is aggressive and will generate lots of heat. As a result, I tend to limit the use of my small grinder to keeping garden tools in shape.

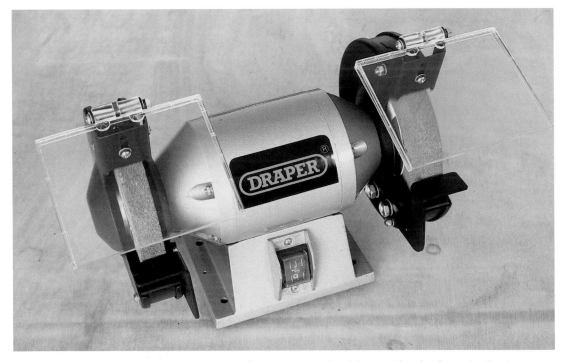

ABOVE Cheap 6in (152mm) grinders are supplied with hard aluminium-oxide wheels. Such wheels are very coarse and of limited use because of the likelihood of overheating an edge. However, they are ideal for robust items like gardening tools and green woodworking tools.

ABOVE This half-speed grinder will reduce the amount of heat build-up and make the grinding process easier to control.

Standard-speed dry grinders can be improved greatly by upgrading the wheels. This will allow for a much more refined finish. However, designed specifically for the turner, half-speed grinders are available which run at 1425 rpm. This slower speed combined with a white or pink wheel (see page 80) gives much better control – a major concern when frequent sharpening is required.

Wet grinders

Wet grinders have either a slow-running motor or some form of reducing gear to decrease the speed of the wheel. They are usually fitted with a soft wheel that can produce a very fine finish, and water runs continually over the surface of the stone, flushing away any unwanted particles and keeping the blade cool. Several models are available, but they all fall into two distinct groups: vertical and horizontal.

Models with vertical wheels look like conventional grinders. The grinding wheel runs in a bath of water and soaks up the water like a sponge. Horizontal models have a trickle feed that constantly supplies water to the grinding surface. Water levels need to be monitored, as evaporation can be quite high. Also, it does not take long

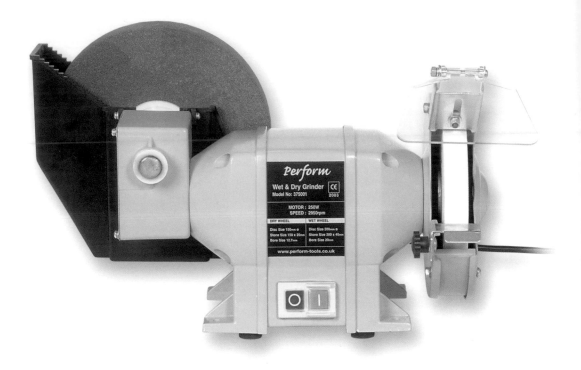

ABOVE A grinder that can run both wet and dry can offer the best of both worlds.

for a thick layer of sludge to collect at the bottom of the water reservoir. This should be cleaned out at the end of each sharpening session.

Although these machines are sold with jigs so that they can be used for a range of applications, they were originally designed with the cabinetmaker in mind and are ideal for sharpening wide-bladed bench tools. Because they were developed for such a specific purpose, some practical problems need to be highlighted.

As wet grinders run so slowly (around 50–100rpm), they tend to be supplied with wheels in which the grit is held in a weak (or 'soft') bond (see page 79). This allows spent grit to detach easily, which in turn prevents the wheel from becoming clogged (or 'glazed'). This is fine for wide-bladed tools – the pressure applied during grinding is spread evenly across the wheel's surface and wear is kept to a minimum. However, when grinding narrower blades and small gouges the pressure applied to the stone is much more focused. The grit will tend to be removed prematurely from these areas, creating an uneven surface. If your intention is to use this type of grinder for sharpening narrow edged tools, it is, therefore, worth considering a different wheel with a harder bond.

ⓒFOCUS ON:

Grading Blocks

ⓒFOCUS ON:

Grading Blocks

The Tormek water-cooled grinder has only one grinding stone – the second wheel is made of leather and used for fine honing and polishing. Instead, a special stone-grading block can be used to 'convert' the grinding wheel from fine to coarse by filling or opening the grain. This process takes about 15–20 seconds, and because the block fills as well as removes material from the stone, the process does not significantly reduce the life of the wheel. The grading block can also be used to reactivate a glazed wheel surface.

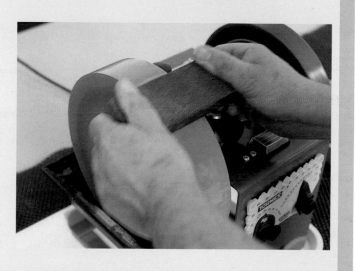

ABOVE Probably the most well-known slow-speed wet grinder: the Tormek. The left-hand wheel is the grinding stone; the smaller wheel on the right is for honing.

RIGHT Using a grading block to convert the grinding wheel is easy.

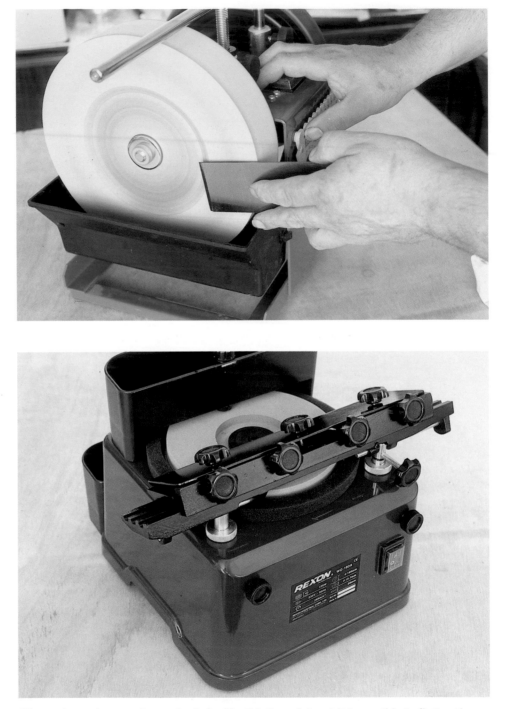

When using a slow-running wet grinder like this Tormek (**TOP**) it is possible to flatten the back of a tool – in this case a plane iron – on the sides of the wheel. This is not possible on a faster-moving wheel. Alternatively, this Rexon horizontal grinder (**ABOVE**) is ideal for honing long, straight blades.

There is one major disadvantage with wet grinders (and waterstones): water. Wet grinding and honing is messy, although with care this is controllable and the resultant edge can be superb.

With horizontal wet grinders, sharpening is carried out on what would be the side of the stone on a conventional grinder. This will produce a flat grind on a wide blade and is ideal for sharpening planer knives and the like. However, narrow-bladed tools are likely to dig into the wheel, or be 'rolled' by the action, and produce a less than satisfactory edge.

Slow-speed wet grinders are renowned for the capacity to produce an ultra-fine finish, and their slow speed and soft wheels means that it is virtually impossible to build up any heat. On the face of it, this may sound like the answer to all the problems associated with grinding an edge, and to some extent this is true – you can sharpen just about anything on a wet-stone grinder. However, other methods may be more suitable in some instances.

TECHNIQUE:

Hollow Grinding

Conventional grinders produce a ground surface that is concave, which is a reflection of the curvature of the wheel. This is known as a 'hollow grind' or 'hollow bevel'. There is much debate about the desirability of a hollow bevel, as opposed to a flat bevel. On the plus side, a hollow bevel can be hand honed quickly and accurately – less material comes into contact with the stone, and the shape of a hollow bevel is inherently stable, minimizing the tendency of the blade to rock during honing. On the other hand, a concave bevel undercuts the edge, making it weaker. The amount of undercut that is produced will relate directly to the diameter of the grinding wheel that has been used to form the bevel.

A popular method of working is to hollow grind the primary bevel and then add a secondary bevel. This helps to avoid a weak edge, while still reducing your sharpening time. However, to accommodate those who insist on a flat grind, some water-cooled grinders are set to a horizontal configuration, which enables the sharpening to be carried out on what would be the side of the stone on a conventional machine.

TECHNIQUE:

Hollow Grinding

2:3 Grinding wheels

By far the most important developments in artificial abrasives were made at the end of the nineteenth century. Until then, the only manmade grinding wheels available were manufactured using abrasive emery powder mixed with potter's clay.

In 1893, Edward Goodrich Acheson patented a process for the manufacture of carborundum (silicon carbide), a very fine artificial abrasive that is still widely used today. This was followed in 1897 by the development of artificial corundum (aluminium oxide). (Although both are generally grey in colour, carborundum grinding wheels should not be confused with the coarse artificial corundum wheels that are normally fitted to cheaper grinders.)

Today, grinding wheels are manufactured from a variety of sophisticated materials, including ceramics and industrial diamond, as well as a number of more common abrasives.

Conventional abrasives

Regardless of what material they are made from, conventional grinding wheels all consist of an abrasive held in a binder. As a tool is sharpened, the abrasive is chipped away, creating fresh cutting edges. Once the grain of abrasive is worn out it detaches from the binder, revealing new grit underneath. The rate at which this happens can be controlled by varying the strength of the bond and the type of abrasive used.

The array of grinding wheels presented to the market is mind-boggling. They come in various colours and materials, and in order to make an informed decision as to what to buy, some understanding of the composition of different types of wheel needs to be acquired. The key characteristics of grinding wheels are identified by a series of code numbers and letters, and this system is outlined in the panel opposite. However, when considering wheels with an aluminium-oxide grit, which is particularly well suited to woodworking tools, another helpful way to break them down is in terms of colour.

Grey

The wheels that come with cheap grinders are usually too coarse to be used for sharpening woodworking tools with any degree of finesse. These grey wheels generally have a very coarse grain and cut with such aggression that the heat build-up is too rapid to be of much use when sharpening relatively delicate tools. Closer grained aluminium-oxide wheels are far more suited to producing the sort of edge required for woodworking. They are available in myriad grades, hardness, shapes and sizes. Some wheels have recessed centres so that a wider cutting surface can be obtained on a grinder with a short arbour, providing the guards can accommodate the extra width.

KEY POINT

KEY POINT

Although the abrasive action of a conventional grinding wheel is provided by the grit, it is the bond used to hold this together that determines whether a stone is described as 'hard' or 'soft'.

ABOVE A coarse grey wheel.

FOCUS ON:

Grinding-wheel Codes

A huge range of different grinding wheels is available, and these can vary widely in terms of bond strength, grit size, density and so on. So how do you pick the right one? To simplify matters, a standard code is used to measure the key characteristics of any given wheel. Although manufacturers use some specifications that are unique to their brand, the following variables are set to an established ISO (International Standards Organization) code.

A	100	J	8	V
Abrasive	Grain size	Grade	Structure	Bond type

Abrasive

This identifies the type of abrasive (or 'grit') used. The most common abrasives are:
A – aluminium oxide (corundum)
C – silicon carbide (carborundum)
D – diamond

Grain size

The grit can be used in different grain sizes. Although most tool grinding is carried out using grit that fits into a medium band of 60 to 120, the scale ranges from 8 to 600 and breaks down into:

8–24 (coarse)
30–60 (medium)
70–180 (fine)
220–600 (very fine)

Grade

Although the type and density of grit can vary, the 'hard' or 'soft' description applied to grinding wheels refers to the bond used. The degree of hardness is indicated by a code letter ranging from A to Z. It is unusual for a code to be much lower (i.e. softer) than D or E, while a Z classification would indicate a very hard bond indeed. You could have various grades of wheel to suit different tasks, but an I or J will suffice as a general-purpose wheel. Use this as a starting point and adjust to a softer grade (lower letter) if the wheel becomes glazed, or a harder one (higher letter) if it erodes excessively.

Structure

As well as the grain size, the relative spacing of the grit in a grinding wheel can also be varied. The scale generally runs from 1 (dense) up to 15 (open). A dense structure is hard wearing, but is more prone to heat build-up and glazing. More open structures, on the other hand, tend to be cooler running because of the reduced friction.

Bond

A single letter is used to represent specific bond types. The most common are:
V – vitrified
B – resin
R – rubber
E – shellac

ABOVE White wheels cut much cooler than grey wheels, helping to prevent the edge from overheating, especially when used on a slow-speed dry grinder.

White

White wheels are made from pure colourless aluminium oxide. These will cut cooler than grey wheels and are far more suited to the needs of the woodworker. At normal grinding speeds these wheels will still heat up the tool fairly quickly, thereby necessitating frequent quenching. The half-speed grinder was developed with this problem in mind, and can go a long way to limiting the problem.

Red/pink

If chromium oxide is added during the manufacturing process, the aluminium oxide that forms the grit will take on a red tint. The finished wheel can be various shades of red or pink, depending on the amount added. Other than changing the colour, which is a useful by-product acting as an indicator of its presence, chromium oxide will alter the crystalline structure of the aluminium-oxide grit, making it break away differently and enhancing the sharpening effect. After the manufacturer has optimized the chromium content, and used a suitable bond, the end result is a wheel that wears much less quickly than a white wheel.

Pink wheels in particular are a good all-round option – as well as holding their shape well, they cut cooler than both the red and white alternatives. They are, therefore, ideal when the requirement is to sharpen a tool frequently while working, as it is easier to avoid overheating the edge. Some versions can also be used on wet grinders.

ABOVE Pink wheels provide a good general-purpose option – they cut cooler than both grey and white wheels, and some versions can be used on wet grinders.

Microcrystalline sintered abrasives

Microcrystalline sintered abrasives are manufactured in an entirely different way to traditional abrasives. The major difference is in the way in which the grit is formed: conventional grit is formed in a furnace, while microcrystalline grit is precipitated from a gel using the latest ceramic technology. More important, however, is the effect that this has on how the grit works during grinding.

As discussed earlier, the grit on conventional wheels consists of individual grains that fracture during grinding to create sharp cutting edges, and eventually detach from the bond to reveal fresh grit underneath. The problem with this is that until the dull edge breaks down and splits away, it rubs against the tool. This friction increases heat build-up in the tool without any useful (i.e. sharpening) effect.

Microcrystalline grit, on the other hand, is made up of tiny clumps of hundreds of small crystals (microcrystalline literally means 'composed of microscopic crystals'). These break down progressively during grinding, keeping the grit sharp at all times and reducing friction to a minimum. Consequently, sintered wheels cut faster and cooler than conventional abrasives, and last up to five times longer than a white wheel. Another advantage is the quality of the finish – because the active cutting grit is so fine, the surface finish is much smoother, reducing (or even eliminating) the need for honing.

KEY POINT

Acclaimed by some to be the ultimate dry-grinding solution for woodworkers, sintered wheels have a very fine crystalline structure that sharpens quickly and smoothly without excessive heating.

FOCUS ON:

Superabrasives

The term 'superabrasive' is applied to the new generation of sophisticated abrasive materials, usually CBN (cubic Boron Nitride) or industrial diamond. While superabrasives offer 'super' performance and are very hard wearing, the more conventional forms of abrasive (especially the latest microcrystalline sintered grinding wheels) are more than adequate when it comes to sharpening woodworking tools.

FOCUS ON:

Superabrasives

KEY POINT

2:4 Choosing the right set-up

Although powered grinders are sold with a wide range of
accessories to suit individual tools, some general practical points
need to be highlighted in advance. This generally involves choosing
the right grinder/wheel combination for the job in hand, whether
basic grinding or fine honing.

If, for example, a plane iron is sharpened on a stone that is too hard,
the surface will become clogged with debris (or 'glazed') because
the grit will not be eroded by the sharpening action. This can be
detrimental to the edge due to the excessive heat that a glazed
wheel will generate. To prevent this from happening, the wheels
used on wet grinders, such as the Tormek, have a soft bond. This
allows even the relatively low pressure created when grinding large,
flat blades to remove spent grit easily.

ABOVE Changing the wheels for a more appropriate composition will make a huge improvement to a cheap grinder (see page 104 for step-by-step instructions on how to carry this procedure out).

(FOCUS ON:

Narrow Tools

(FOCUS ON:

Narrow Tools

Narrow blades and small gouges are highly susceptible to heat build-up and should not be sharpened on a basic high-speed dry grinder. Wet grinders cut much cooler, but narrow tools tend to remove the grit of their soft wheels prematurely, and this excessive stone wear can produce unwanted grooves in the surface.

Fortunately, it is possible to flatten (or 'true') an out-of-shape wheel using a diamond truing tool. However, it may be worth considering a different set-up if you mainly work with narrow edged tools. For example, some pink aluminium-oxide wheels (see page 80) can be used on wet grinders and make an excellent hard-wearing alternative.

ABOVE A grinder stand is useful, especially for the turner, as the stand can be positioned within easy reach of the turning position.

A Woodturner's Set-up

Most woodworkers will use grinders from time to time to create or reset a primary bevel angle, while the final finish is maintained by hand. However, things are slightly different for turners. Here the aim is to get the best edge possible, straight from the grinder, with a minimum of fuss. Rapid, light and frequent sharpening is required, and the edge should be touched up continually as the job progresses.

The ideal situation is to have a grinder within reach of the working position, and this is where a grinder stand comes into its own. A wet grinder may seem like a good option, but its slow cutting speed would be frustrating given the frequent sharpening required. For this reason, most turners prefer to do all their touching up freehand on dry grinders. A slow-speed dry grinder or a microcrystalline sintered wheel will help limit heat build-up and give a good finish even without honing.

KEY POINT

Carving, turning and cabinetmaking tools all have different requirements when it comes to sharpening. Think carefully about what combination of grinder and wheel will best suit your needs.

KEY POINT

2:5 Jigs and tool rests

There are nearly as many jigs and tool rests available as there are
wheels. As with sharpening by hand, opinions are divided on
whether or not it is desirable to use a sharpening aid to hold and
guide the tool while grinding. It really depends on what you are
trying to achieve. Some manufacturers try to be all things to all
people and offer a jig to sharpen everything, from the finest of
carving tools to the heavy blades of felling axes and everything in
between. In fairness they do, for the most part, work. Having said
that, in some cases there is a better way.

Probably the most useful thing to add to a grinder is an adjustable
tool rest. All grinders come with some sort of tool rest – even the
cheapest of models have a simple one incorporated – but the small
rest supplied with the majority of grinders is only just adequate.
There are several to chose from. Some are simply an adjustable
platform, while others will accommodate a whole range of add-ons
(such as clamps) and facilitate the sharpening of a range of tools.

ABOVE A wide range of guides and jigs makes the Tormek one of the most versatile wet-grinding systems available.

ABOVE This two-in-one sharpening guide can be used as a honing guide on a bench stone or, by removing the roller, it can double as a tool clamp on a grinder.

KEY POINT

Sharpening aids create a stable platform for accurate grinding and sharpening. Any guide used should be fully adjustable, allowing you to set different angles and to slide the blade continually back and forth across the wheel.

Straight blades

Grinding chisel blades and plane irons is quite straightforward, as is sharpening most straight blades. The trick here is to maintain a constant angle to the tangent of the wheel. A simple clamp secured across the blade at a pre-set distance from the edge will determine the grinding angle, and allow the edge to slide back and forth across the wheel. Holding the tool by hand between the thumb and forefinger will work equally well. Care must be taken to ensure that the grind is square to the sides of the tool, so that the bevel is not skewed.

Curved blades

When it comes to grinding and profiling gouges, things become more inventive. Specialist jigs designed for specific tasks are available – which one(s) you choose will depend on the tools you intend to sharpen. For example, a fingernail jig can be set to accommodate a wide range of profiles and sizes and is ideal for holding spindle gouges, which are notoriously hard to sharpen by hand.

⟮TECHNIQUE:

Getting the Angle Right

The type of tool you are sharpening and the use to which it is put will dictate the grinding angle you are trying to achieve. In order to grind the tool to that specific angle, an accurate means of presenting it to the grindstone needs to be established. Most dedicated sharpening systems – like that produced by Tormek – have a range of accessories, each with fully tested procedures put down in black and white for the user to follow. But all sorts of angle finders and setting jigs are available and they all have their own merits. The various methods of establishing the grinding angles will be covered on a tool-by-tool basis in part three (see page 91).

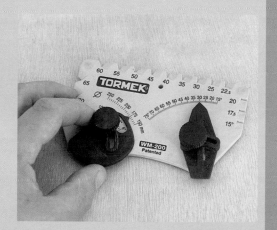

ABOVE Setting the grinding angle is easy. Tormek's adjustable angle-setting guide even allows for wheel wear – but first you must decide what is appropriate for the individual tool and the job it will be used for.

⟮TECHNIQUE:

Getting the Angle Right

Part 3:
Sharpening in Practice

3:1 Honing by hand

There is generally a misconception that only the novice uses a honing guide. However, it is not shameful to be seen using one; indeed, I would recommend that you do. I always set the primary bevels on my own chisels with a honing guide, although a quick 'touch up' is usually done by hand.

It is of course possible to carry out the entire process by hand, and a lot of people do. Honing by hand is all about 'feel'. You must familiarize yourself with the method of holding the chisel and how to maintain that angle.

This is something that will only come with time and practice.

The most useful application of honing by hand is to touch up an edge during the course of a job. Perfecting this will save time that would otherwise have to be spent fiddling about with setting a honing guide for what is only a few passes. This is also where the micro bevel pays dividends, as any re-sharpening is only carried out on this small area. The new edge is formed quickly because there is little material to remove. All that will be required is a few strokes over the finest stone or paper that was used to establish the bevel, and a couple on the back to remove the burr.

Don't wait until an edge is too dull to work efficiently. As soon as the performance drops off in the slightest way, re-establish it. Continually maintaining the edge will mean that your tools are performing at their best, making your work easier and more accurate.

ABOVE Keeping it sharp during the course of the job will improve the quality of your work and save time in the long run.

As the micro bevel is honed and re-honed repeatedly, the top edge will move up the primary bevel. Eventually this will increase the size of the micro bevel to such an extent that it will be worth re-grinding the primary bevel and establishing a new micro bevel.

Fear of ruining all that hard work getting the chisel sharp in the first place is one of the reasons that freehand honing is often avoided – but you will not ruin anything. Most of the work in establishing a good edge to a tool goes into preparing the back, and hand honing the bevels will not alter that. Once you have tried it a few times you will be amazed just how easy and effective it really is. The following step-by-step sequences show techniques for honing a chisel by hand, but the same basic principles can be applied to any straight-edged tool.

ABOVE Quick and easy: touching up the edge of a chisel freehand on a bench stone.

How to hone by hand

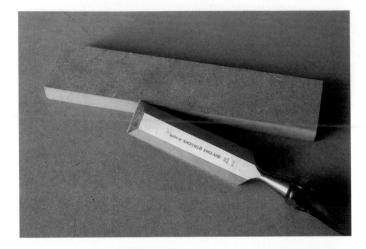

1 A block of MDF makes a good dummy stone to practise holding and honing techniques without the risk of causing any damage to the chisel or the stone. Select a wide chisel to start with, as this will have a larger surface area and be less likely to rock from side to side.

2 Rest the chisel on the block, with the heel in contact with the surface. Hold the chisel with your thumbs underneath and the fore and second fingers of each hand arranged on the back over the bevel.

3 With your thumbs under the chisel, fore and second fingers above, lift the handle end of the chisel with the thumbs while applying pressure to the area directly behind the bevel with the fingers. The heel of the bevel will act as a fulcrum and the chisel will sit flat on the bevel.

4 This is the position that needs to be maintained to keep the bevel flat. The chisel should be worked over the surface in such a manner as to maintain the most even wear pattern possible. (The practice of using the surface evenly is far more important when sharpening narrower bladed tools.)

5 Lifting the chisel higher will lift the heel off the surface, and the chisel will be resting on the tip of the bevel. Honing at this angle will produce the micro bevel.

6 Once you feel confident, have a go on a real stone. Don't be discouraged if the bevel is not perfect first time – look carefully at the result and try again. The hardest thing to achieve is the flatness. Any lifting or dropping of the chisel's angle will result in a convex surface. Locking the hands and wrists and making the movement from the shoulders and elbows will help. Good results will come with time.

Maintaining an edge by hand

1 Maintain the edge on the finest grit used to produce it.

2 Here, a chisel is being honed on a sheet of 1500-grit silicon-carbide abrasive paper; a super-fine stone could also be used, if that is your preference. Rest the top of the bevel on the abrasive surface and lift the chisel until the primary bevel is in contact with the abrasive.

3 Now lift the chisel a few degrees more so that it is resting on the micro bevel and make two strokes of the stone, concentrating on maintaining a constant angle. This should produce a fine burr on the back of the blade.

4 Inspect the micro bevel. If this is the first re-hone, that is probably enough to re-establish the edge. Don't hone more than you need – an extra 'lick' will not make the tool any sharper if a burr is being produced. Each honing extends the micro bevel, reducing the number of sharpenings possible before re-grinding becomes necessary.

5 Remove the burr. It is important that the chisel is held perfectly flat while doing this. Also, always lift the edge of the tool clear of the surface first to avoid damaging the freshly honed edge.

3:2 High-speed dry grinders

As they are supplied, cheap high-speed dry grinders are not of much use when it comes to sharpening fine woodworking tools.

Most of them come equipped with very coarse, hard wheels that will quickly overheat the edge of a delicate chisel, and the tool rests will be inadequate for curved edged tools like carving gouges. (See part two, page 63, for more details on high-speed grinders and grinding wheels.)

By changing the wheels and adding new tool rests and jigs, a cheap model can be transformed into a useful workshop machine.

However, there are some important considerations to be taken into account when re-equipping a high-speed grinder, and the following step-by-step instructions (see overleaf) provide a useful guide to the process.

Upgrading a budget-priced 6in (152mm) grinder

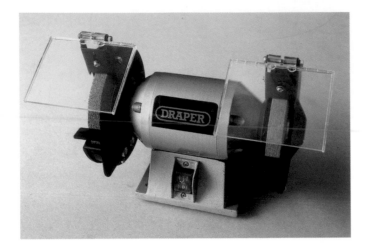

1 This Draper 6in grinder is supplied with the usual coarse grey wheels. Changing them for better quality wheels will improve the usefulness of the machine to the woodworker. The wheels can cost more than the machine, but the investment will pay dividends in terms of ease of use and quality of sharpening.

2 The choice of wheel is a balance between cost and practical use. In this example, this grinder is to be fitted with a pair of wider wheels, one pink with a reduced thickness centre and one blue without a reduction in thickness.

3 The wheels supplied with this grinder are ¾in (20mm) wide. A broader wheel will give more support to wider tools, will be less susceptible to uneven wear, and is easier to dress. Fitting wider wheels to a standard grinder is a straightforward operation. There is usually enough room within the guards to accommodate the extra width; the problem is normally the length of the shaft, or rather the lack of it.

4 Either the wheel needs to have a recessed centre, as this pink wheel…

5 …or narrower flanges can be substituted for the standard ones, as here, to accommodate this full-thickness blue wheel.

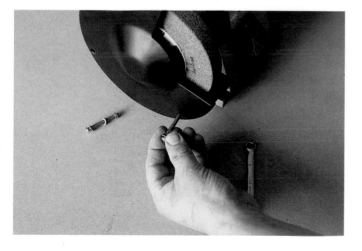

6 With the grinder turned off and unplugged from the power socket, remove the guard by loosening the three machine screws, nuts and washers that hold the case together.

Upgrading a budget-priced 6in (152mm) grinder

7 The screws that hold the inadequate tool rest to the guard should also be removed as they can make contact with the wheel if tightened up without the tool rest in place.

8 Loosen the securing nut on the end of the shaft, remembering that as you look at the grinder, the left-hand shaft is most likely to have a reverse (left-hand) thread.

9 Remove the original wheel. The flanges will probably be stuck to the labels, which will act as a cushion between the abrasive of the wheel and the flanges. These cushions, whether doubling up as labels or not, are called 'blotters'.

10 If the flanges are stuck to the blotters, do not try levering them off with a screwdriver or similar metal object, as this may cause damage to the flange or wheel. Instead, insert a piece of ½in (12.7mm) dowel into the centre of the flange and break the bond by turning the dowel out of alignment.

11 Clean up the surface of the flanges by removing any debris from the old wheels. The flanges need to be as true as possible – any lumps or bumps on the surface will cause stress on the grinding wheel and this may result in excessive side to-side wobble.

12 Before fitting a new grinding wheel, check it for any damage or cracks. If there are no visible signs of damage, pass a pencil through the hole and lightly tap the wheel with a piece of wood. The wheel should 'ring' like a piece of sound pottery. If it does not and the sound is dull, the wheel is likely to be cracked and should not be used.

Upgrading a budget-priced 6in (152mm) grinder

13 After it has been established that the wheel is sound, reassemble the wheel and cleaned flanges onto its shaft. Lightly tighten the nut.

14 With the grinder still disconnected from the power supply, spin the wheel by hand to check for excessive side-to-side play (in excess of 1mm). If this is present it is probably because the flanges are distorted or foreign objects are trapped between the blotters and flanges. Try re-seating the flanges at 90° to each other or adding an extra blotter (cut from thin card) to the motor side of the wheel. Under no circumstances try to dress the side of the wheel in an attempt to eliminate wobble. Dressing the wheel can rectify front-to-back play, if necessary, once the guards and tool rests are in place.

15 Assemble the guards back onto the machine and turn the wheel by hand to check that nothing is rubbing or in any way fouling the wheel. This wheel is ready to be powered up. On initial start-up, always stand to the side of the machine and let the wheel run for a couple of minutes before putting it to use.

16 Fitting a non-recessed wheel is a similar procedure to that of fitting a recessed wheel. The guards, wheel and flanges are detached from the grinder, and the original flanges are removed and machined to a narrower profile, or replaced with thinner ones if available.

17 There is a wide range of commercial tool rests available, some for general-purpose use and others designed to perform a specific task. This grinder is to be fitted with a Veritas grinder tool rest and honing jigs on the right-hand side of the machine, plus a wide general-purpose rest with mitre slot and gauge on the other.

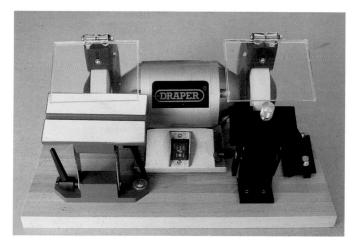

18 Both of these tools are designed to be bolted or screwed down in front of the grinder, either in a permanent position at the end of a bench or in a dedicated area. As few of us will have the space to dedicate an area specifically for grinding, the portable approach is taken here by bolting the grinder and the rests to a substantial piece of board. The board can be clamped to a bench when required.

3:3 Chisels

Over the past 30-odd years I have always sharpened new tools straight out of the box without giving it a second thought. At school I was taught that new edged tools were supplied prepared for sharpening, ready for the craftsman to hone to an edge.

It had not occurred to me to impart this basic piece of information to anyone else, until I realized that if I had not have followed woodworking at school, I'm not sure where else I would have gained this fundamental piece of knowledge. It is unusual for hand tools to come with instructions of any kind; it is even less likely that manufacturers of mass-market chisels and planes are going to state that their tools need sharpening before use.

The fact is that most chisels get put straight to use without any preparation whatsoever. A great deal of these will never get sharpened again. The manufacturers supply tools with a ground bevel that will 'cut' as sold, and the casual user will not want to sharpen a new chisel. However, with a bit of careful sharpening, that standard, off-the-shelf tool can be transformed into something that will perform entirely differently.

The usual rules apply when it comes to buying chisels: the cheaper the tool, the more work you will have to do to get it to perform. This does not mean that a cheap chisel will perform as well as an expensive one if you spend a week honing it! What is does mean is that, within the limitations imposed by the quality of the tool's construction, the maximum possible performance can be achieved.

General requirements

The first thing to do is to flatten an area across the back of the cutting edge. In an ideal world the whole back should be flat, but with a cheap tool the machining tolerances will mean that this is not a practical option. It is most important that the area directly behind the ground bevel is as flat as possible. This is where the two surfaces are going to meet in order to create the cutting edge as the blade is continually sharpened.

The process of sharpening new chisels is the same regardless of type: the factory grind needs to be refined and a cutting bevel established at a suitable angle. Care needs to be taken when grinding narrow chisels to keep the bevel square, especially with bevel-edged chisels. These have less material in contact with the sharpening surface and so have a tendency to rock from side to side on the top, narrow heel of the bevel.

Extra care needs to be exercised when sharpening narrow blades. These impart much more focused grinding pressure than wide blades, which will spread the load over a larger area. When sharpening a narrow blade by hand it is very easy to score a stone or dig the tip into the surface if the tool is lifted or tipped from side to side. Make very light passes until a flat area of removal is evident. This is especially important when using a waterstone, as they can be quite soft.

Adapting the skills

What is good for one can apply to the other. The step-by-step examples that follow show various methods of sharpening chisels, but each method can be applied to all similar tools – i.e. a plane blade can be sharpened using a method shown for a chisel, and vice versa.

When sharpening bench tools of any type, whether chisels or plane irons, it is worth spending time making the backs as near perfect as possible, as you will only have to do it once. All subsequent honing is carried out on the bevels.

In all cases I have honed and polished all surfaces to a flat-grind, mirror finish. If you prefer to maintain a hollow grind, skip the stages relating to honing the primary bevel and just produce a micro bevel onto the hollow grind.

FOCUS ON:

Choosing the Right Edge Angle

Chisels are normally supplied with a primary grind of 25°. This is a fair compromise from the manufacturers – they have to put some kind of grind on there. The trouble is that chisels have such varied usage that the range of grinds and honing angles is endless.

A finely honed paring chisel with a cutting bevel of 20° will slice through soft wood, render a silky finish and hold a good edge. These chisels are designed to take very light shavings from joints using only hand pressure. If you were to try cutting a mortise with one, the edge would crumple and the chisel would most likely wedge itself firmly in the wood. In order to strengthen the edge, the angle needs to be increased. Mortise chisels are situated at the other end of the finesse scale, supporting heavy solid blades, chunky handles and even a metal protector to stop the handles splitting under the stress of constant bombardment of the joiner's mallet.

An angle of 30° or more is the normal recommendation for a general-purpose mortise chisel, with some heavy-duty chisels supporting cutting angles of as much as 40°.

The grinding and honing angles of chisels is a huge subject, and for most part is a matter of personal preference. When grinding chisels for general use, I always grind at 25° and hone a few degrees steeper at 30°.

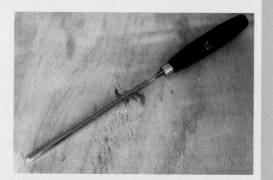

ABOVE The finesse of a paring chisel.

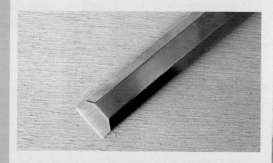

ABOVE Most bench tools are supplied with a 25° bevel. For delicate work, this 25° angle can be honed and polished, and a fine secondary bevel added at 26 or 27°.

ABOVE A mortise chisel will have a coarser cutting angle, starting at around 30° and sometimes increasing to 40° or more.

Sharpening a set of general-purpose chisels

1 A set of Irwin/Marples chisels. This box is typical of middle-of-the-road, everyday chisel sets. The chisels are made to a good standard and are ready for the user to tune to his or her needs.

2 The finish is of good standard but now needs to be refined and polished in order to remove the grinding marks.

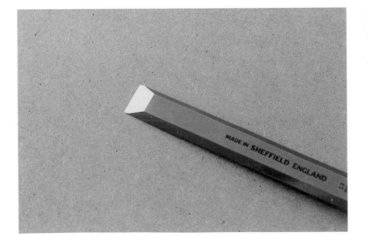

3 The primary bevel is usually ground to 25° on a general-purpose set like this. A simple angle checker will confirm this.

4 Start the preparation by flattening the back. Here, the process is being carried out on a coarse oilstone, which has been primed with honing oil.

5 The process will start to remove material at the high spots.

6 Continue to work the chisel until material is being removed evenly from the entire area to be flattened. On a chisel, this is the area behind the bevel that is to be sharpened and both the outer sides. A hollow in the centre is not a problem.

Sharpening a set of general-purpose chisels

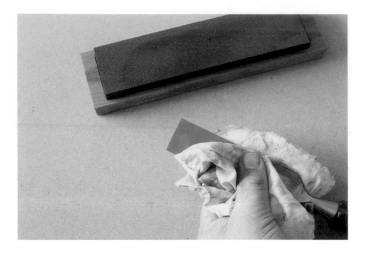

7 Clean the chisel when moving from one grit to another to avoid cross contamination.

8 It is also good practice to wipe the stone clean after each use.

9 Once the back has been flattened, move to a medium-grit stone and reduce the size of the scratches made by the coarse stone used for initial flattening.

10 Final flattening on a fine stone will reduce the size of the scratches still further.

11 A final option is to polish the back to a mirror finish using a fine cream abrasive. It is worth making the effort on the back, as once it has been flattened you should not need to do it again unless it becomes damaged in some way.

Sharpening a set of general-purpose chisels

12 Now the back is flat and polished, attention can be turned to the factory-ground bevel. This will almost certainly be 25°, as it is on the chisels in this set. The grinding will be slightly concave (hollow) because it will have been produced by a grinding wheel.

13 There is great debate as to whether a hollow or flat grind to the primary bevel is desirable or not (see page 75). This is something only you can decide upon. Try both and in time your own preference will show through.

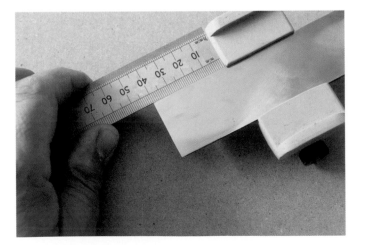

14 To flatten the primary bevel, set the chisel in a honing guide. I always use a guide for this procedure – as long as the chisel is set in the guide correctly, the resultant finished bevel will be accurate and, just as importantly, easily replicated.

15 Honing the bevel on a medium-grit stone will start to remove material from the high points. With a hollow-ground chisel this will be at the top and bottom of the bevel.

16 Continue the honing process until material is being removed evenly over the entire face of the bevel. The bevel is now flat.

17 Moving down to a finer stone will refine the surface.

Sharpening a set of general-purpose chisels

18 A final polish using a cream abrasive will give the surface a mirror finish.

19 Re-polish the back to remove any burr still remaining.

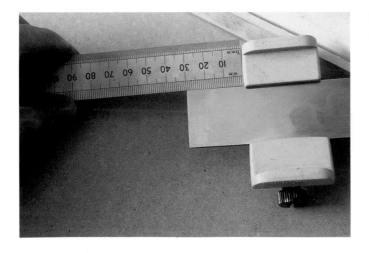

20 For general use, apply a secondary bevel of 30° by resetting the chisel in the jig.

21 A few strokes on the fine stone will establish the secondary bevel.

22 A final polish and a couple of strokes of the back to remove the burr and the new chisel is ready for use.

Sharpening a set of pre-polished chisels using waterstones

1 A set of Kirschen bench chisels. At first glance these chisels appear to be finished to a much higher standard than the Irwin/Marples set. The entire blade has been polished to a mirror finish and the bevel is finely ground to 25°. Unfortunately, the back still needs flattening, although this will require less work than before. The mirror finish shows a distorted reflection, confirming that the back is not flat.

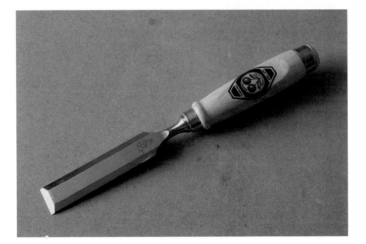

2 Steel that is polished to a mirror finish is susceptible to rust if it is not protected by some kind of water-resistant coating. In use, this would usually be oil of some type. Here, the manufacturer has varnished the whole chisel, blade and all, to keep them looking bright and new for the eventual customer.

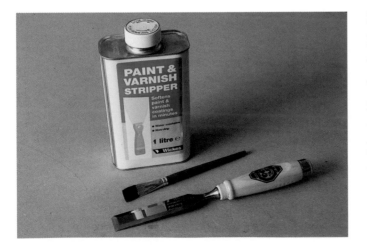

3 The varnish is best removed prior to honing, as it is likely to clog the grain of the sharpening stones. This is easily done with a proprietary paint stripper. Take care not to remove the varnish from the handles, unless you want to refinish them as well. Masking tape will keep any overspill off the handles.

4 Using waterstones can be a messy business. In fact, it is probably the messiest way I know of sharpening. If you can cope with (or control) the mess, this method will produce sharp tools quickly. A stone pond is one method of controlling the water.

5 The coarse and medium-grit stones can be stored in the water providing that the temperature is kept above freezing. This stone pond enables the runners to be inverted and a lid will reduce evaporation and keep the dirt and sawdust out.

6 Fine stones should be allowed to dry out between sharpening sessions. They will then need to be immersed in water for five to ten minutes before the next session in order to recharge the stone.

Sharpening a set of pre-polished chisels using waterstones

7 An alternative to the pond is to mount the stone in a stone clamp and place it on a tray to collect the runoff. The tray is placed on non-slip matting to prevent it from moving while a tool is sharpened.

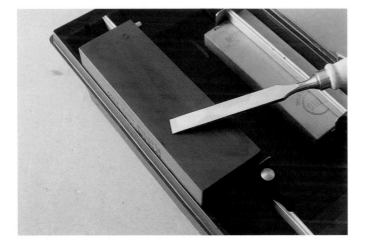

8 Once the stone is stable and charged with water, honing can commence. The backs of the chisels should be checked for flatness by honing them on the medium (1000-grit) waterstone. You will be able to see a difference in the reflection where the stone has been removing material from the chisel.

9 Continue to hone the back until a flat, even grey colour is obtained over the entire back. At this point the removal rate is constant over the entire surface and the back is flat.

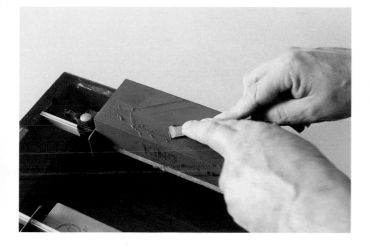

10 Continue to hone for a few strokes, allowing a slurry to build up on the stone. This will reduce the cutting action and reduce the size of the scratches that need to be polished out on the finer stone.

11 Move to a fine stone and polish the back to a shiny finish.

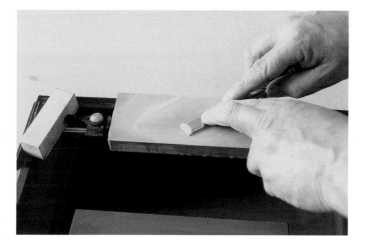

12 Use a Nagura stone to create a slurry on the fine stone for final polishing to a mirror finish.

Sharpening a set of pre-polished chisels using waterstones

13 The back is now flat and polished. A perfect reflection, with no distortion, is the proof.

14 Attention can now turn to the bevel. First measure the grinding angle; this is usually – but not always – 25°.

15 Here we are using the Veritas setting jig to clamp the chisel into the honing guide ready for use.

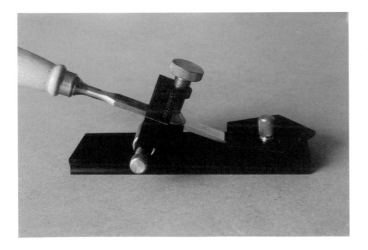

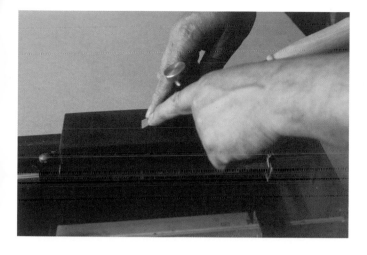

16 Using a medium-grit stone, move the chisel back and forth over the surface, applying moderate pressure to the back of the bevel area. The wider contact area of larger chisels will require more pressure than narrower ones. Use as much of the stone's surface as possible in order to even out the wear.

17 Check the progress after a few strokes. The hollow grind of the chisel's bevel will mean that material is being removed from the toe and heel of the bevel, gradually flattening towards the middle.

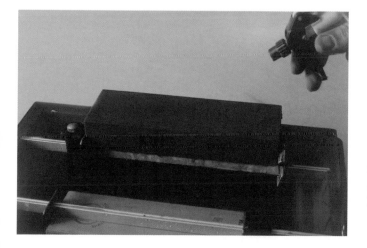

18 Keep the stone free from sludge build-up by rinsing the stone with fresh water at regular intervals. A spray bottle, such as those used for plants, is ideal for this. As the honing process draws to an end, allow the sludge to build up. This will reduce the efficiency of the stone, effectively reducing its cutting grit size and making the final polishing easier (because the scratches will be smaller).

Sharpening a set of pre-polished chisels using waterstones

19 When the removal of material becomes continuous across the bevel, the process has produced a flat grind to the primary bevel. The surface should be a flat grey colour.

20 Without changing any settings, move over to a fine stone and start to polish the bevel in the same sequence as was used to polish the back.

21 A unique feature of the Veritas honing guide is the ability to increase the angle of contact by up to 3°. This means that a micro bevel can be applied to the edge without resetting the clamp.

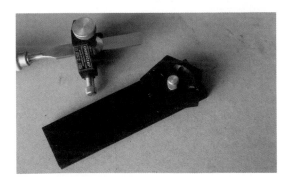

22 If, however, a larger angle is required, say 5°, the chisel will need to be reset in the clamp. This is easy to achieve using the setting jig, and few passes on the fine stone will establish the micro bevel.

23 Remove the burr by passing the back of the chisel up and down a fine stone a couple of times at 90° to the stone. This will cut the burr rather than snapping it off by running the chisel down the stone in the honing orientation.

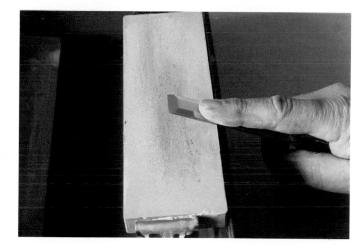

24 Always lift the chisel by raising the edge clear first. This will ensure that rocking on the stone will not damage the newly formed edge.

25 Wipe the chisel clean and apply a coat of protective oil to prevent rust. The chisel is now ready for use.

Renovating an old chisel on a wet grinder

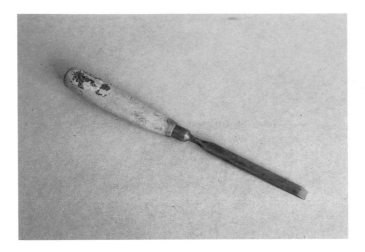

1 This old chisel was purchased second hand for a small outlay. Although it has seen some abuse during its life, it will soon be back in usable condition.

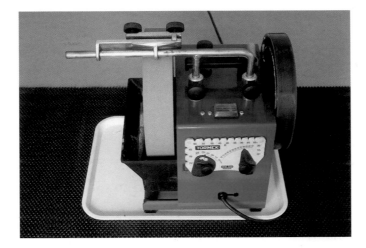

2 No matter what precautions are taken, some of the water will invariably escape the confines of the reservoir. This Tormek wet grinder is standing on a plastic tray, which is in turn standing on a piece of non-slip matting to prevent the tray sliding away during use.

3 First, grade the grinding wheel of a Tormek using a grading block (see page 73). Here, the side of the stone is being opened (i.e. made coarser), ready to flatten the back of the chisel.

4 Using wet-and-dry abrasive paper, remove any rust from the chisel before you start grinding. Rust left on the blade will clog the side of the wheel and be difficult to remove.

5 Hold the back of the blade against the wheel, moving it up and down whilst applying steady pressure. Keep the chisel pointing towards the reservoir. This has nothing to do with the quality of the grind, it stops the excess water from running down your sleeve! Once the chisel has been flattened, the back will be uniform in appearance. At this stage the wheel can be 'converted' back to a fine grade by applying the fine side of the stone grader to the wheel for 15 seconds or so. The back can now be ground to a low polish.

Renovating an old chisel on a wet grinder

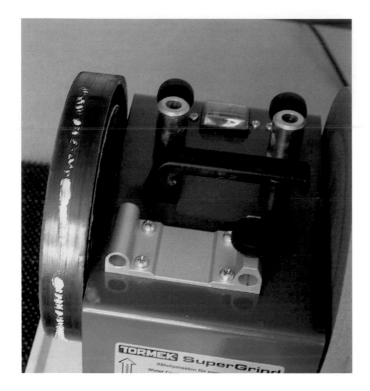

6 Turn the machine around. This ensures that the leather honing wheel is running away from you preventing any risk of the tool digging into the wheel. Charge the honing wheel with a small amount of polishing compound.

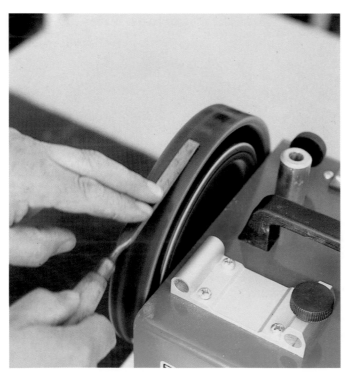

7 Polish the back of the chisel to a mirror finish by moving it back and forth across the top of the charged honing wheel.

8 That neglected chisel has now taken on a totally new lease of life with a perfectly flat mirror finish to its back.

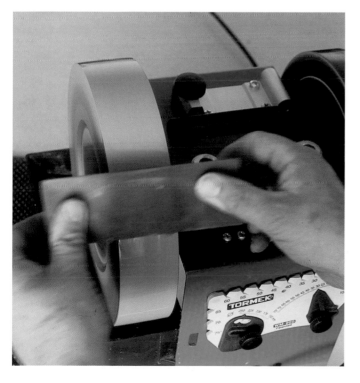

9 Convert the wheel to a coarse grade using the stone grader, making sure that the block is moved from side to side to even out the wear on the block. This will take 15–30 seconds.

Renovating an old chisel on a wet grinder

10 At this stage, it is time to decide how you want to grind your chisel. Tormek maintain that you only need one bevel because the process is so easy that subsequent sharpening will be carried out in the same way. That's fine, but I am of the opinion that a secondary bevel is the way to go. The primary grind is set at 25° using the straight-edge jig and the Tormek angle-setting device.

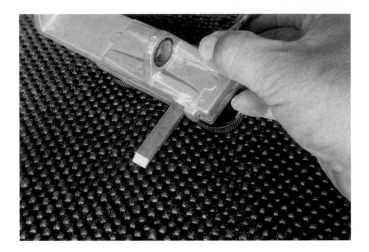

11 Grind the chisel until the new primary bevel is formed. Grade the stone back to fine, and complete the grinding.

12 Polish the bevel on the honing wheel. A little cosmetic polishing of the rest of the chisel can also be undertaken at this stage.

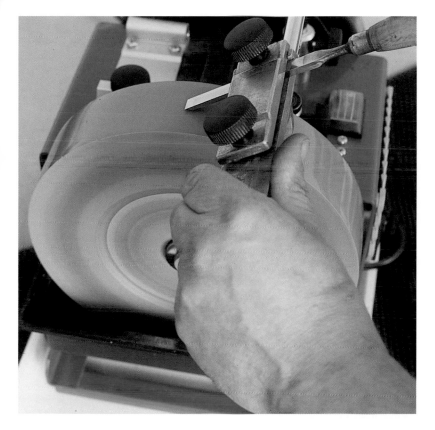

13 Position the chisel back into the straight-edge guide, this time set for the secondary bevel of 30°. One or two passes are all that is required to establish a secondary bevel.

14 Hone the resultant burr off on the honing wheel – and that tired old chisel is ready for work again.

3:4 Plane blades

New plane blades are usually supplied with the primary bevel ground to 25°, the same as is applied to chisels. Except for specialist planes, this is the norm.

The quality of the iron varies considerably, from a thin stamped-out piece of metal, through to a reasonably thick general-purpose iron, and ultimately up to the hand-forged works of art supplied with the high-quality planes made by the specialist makers.

Some really cheap planes have irons that are so flimsy as to be useless, and these should be discarded. There is no point in spending a lot of time grinding and honing an iron that is too thin to stay rigid in use. Some of these cheap planes can be refitted with better quality irons and caps, but most of the time the plane body has so many defects that it is best to avoid these ultra-cheap tools completely.

If you are trying to perfect your sharpening technique, a plane that is of such bad quality will not provide a result that fairly reflects your labours.

ABOVE Checking that the cap iron is flush on the back of the plane iron.

Attention should be paid to the cap iron, where appropriate, to ensure it is seated properly against the back of the iron. This may also need grinding and honing to achieve a gap-free union. Again, it is good policy to smooth off any roughness left after manufacture.

It is also important to ensure that the cutting edge is ground square to the sides of the iron. It is worth checking this using a small engineer's square before starting the sharpening process, as it is not unheard of for the manufacturer's ground edge to be out of square. It is of course possible to compensate for this when re-seating the iron in the plane, but it is far better to start off with something as near perfect as possible.

Honing short blades

The honing guides used for chisels can, for the most part, be used with plane irons. The only restriction is the length, or rather lack of length, of the shorter irons found in some of the special-use planes. Some guides are better suited to these small

ABOVE Checking the edge of the iron is square to the sides.

blades than others. The shorter the projection, the lower the clamp has to be to maintain a similar angle. Stanley's honing guide is specifically designed to handle small blades, and although the intention is for it to be used with larger plane irons and chisels too, the low position of the clamp and the inherent low clamping pressure of the design makes this somewhat impractical.

If you want to hone small plane irons by hand, you may find that there is not always enough material to hold. On these occasions a simple honing stick can be made to hold the iron – in effect making a handle for it. This can be made from a section of hardwood with a slot cut into the end. The short iron can be inserted into this and held in place with a wedge or clamping screw. The design and shape will depend on the iron in question. Special sticks can also be made to ease the honing of skew irons, especially small ones.

ABOVE The Stanley honing guide has a very low profile, making it ideal for short blades.

FOCUS ON:

Flattening the Back

FOCUS ON:

Flattening the Back

Unlike chisels, plane irons do not need their entire back flattened as the sole of the plane is what maintains contact with the timber, not the back of the iron. It is the area directly behind the bevel that is important. This is the area that will become the new edge as the iron is progressively sharpened. Flattening the back can be a laborious job on a plane iron, especially if it is a cheap one – there are times when the blade is so dished or twisted that either a compromise has to be made or the iron substituted for a better-quality item. The flattening process should only need to be done once, so it is worth putting the effort in to get it right.

ABOVE Some cheap plane irons are not manufactured to close-enough tolerances to enable the back to be flattened without it being necessary to remove large amounts of material.

137

Sharpening a new plane iron using abrasive paper

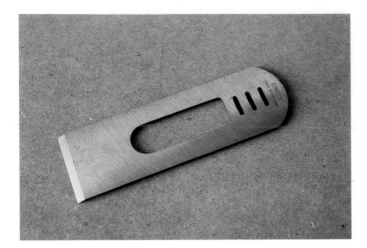

1 This iron is from a Stanley block plane. The ground finish is fairly even, but the back will need to be polished and the primary bevel honed to 25° and polished ready for a 27° micro bevel to be applied.

2 Waterproof silicon-carbide abrasive paper (i.e. wet and dry) is most commonly found in the automotive refinishing trade. The wide range of grits makes it extremely versatile: it is used to smooth fillers and flatten paint, and the finer grades can be used to polish the paint. For woodworking, the coarser grades are ideal for initial grinding of edged tools and the very fine grades will produce a mirror finish.

3 A flat surface onto which the paper can be mounted is required. A piece of plate glass is a good choice. The paper can be cut into strips and mounted with spray mount adhesive.

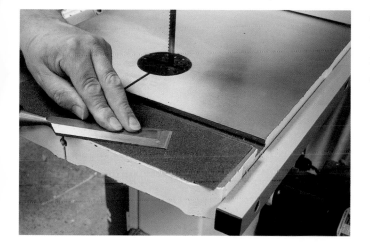

4 An alternative is to tape the paper to the bed of a machine. The band-saw table is a convenient location for a quick touch up of an edge.

5 Start the process by flattening the back on a fairly coarse (240-grit) sheet, until it is flat.

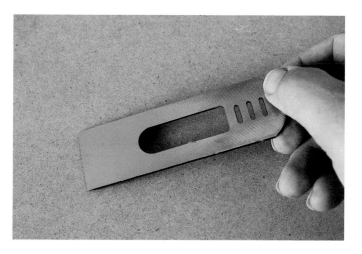

6 The important bit is the area behind the bevel and as far as the slot. This is where sharpening will consume the iron over time. This area will need to be flattened and polished to the best possible finish.

Sharpening a new plane iron using abrasive paper

7 Work your way down through a selection of grits, in fairly even steps. The paper can be worked wet or dry and lubricated with water or oil. I prefer to use it dry, but this means that the paper needs changing more frequently.

8 Alternate the direction of cut as the grits get finer – it will be easier to see whether the surface has been completely honed if the scratches oppose each other.

9 Continue on to the finer grits. Here, the paper is 1500 grit and a mirror finish is produced. Further honing is possible on finer and finer grits, but there is a point at which the structure of the metal used for the iron will start to become coarser than the honing grit. At this point, no further improvement will be accomplished.

10 Now attention is turned to the bevel. The iron is held in a honing guide, and this time an old 'Record Edged Tool Honer 161' is used. This is particularly good for small irons. Although new versions are not currently available, it is fairly common on the second-hand market.

11 Set the iron in the honing guide to produce a 25° primary bevel. This can be set using the Veritas setting jig or a workshop-made template. The honing guide is marked 'PROJECT 1 INCH FOR 30°' (or 25.4mm in metric). As we want 25°, this is not much help. In fact, in this case a projection of about 1¼in (32mm) will give a 25° honing angle.

12 Start the honing process with a grit that will cut vigorously enough to flatten the bevel. However, to avoid making unnecessary work this should be fine enough to sharpen the edge without making deep scratches that will have to be polished back out. Here, the honing is commenced with 400-grit paper.

Sharpening a new plane iron using abrasive paper

13 Once an even removal of material is reached, honing is once again continued down through the grits until a mirror finish is achieved.

14 If the iron is reset to a projection of 1in (25.4mm), the honing angle will be increased to 30°. A slightly longer projection will give the 27° angle required.

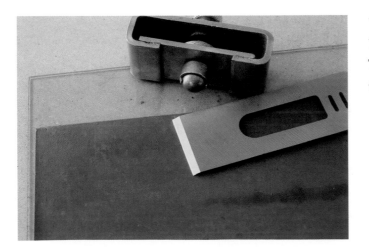

15 Hone a micro bevel, starting with 1200-grit paper, and polish it on 1500 grit. The iron is now ready to be removed from the honing guide.

16 Remove the burr from the iron by rubbing the iron sideways along the finest grit used to polish the back – in this case, 1500 grit.

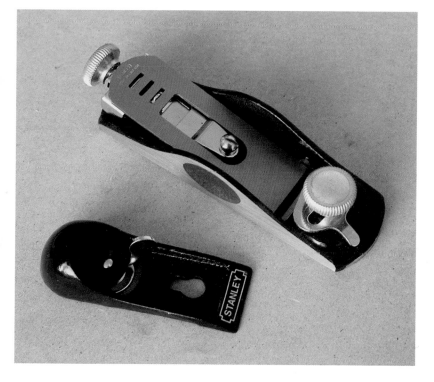

17 The iron is now ready to be reassembled into the plane body.

Re-establishing the primary bevel on an old plane iron

1 This procedure is carried out using a microcrystalline wheel (see page 81), which will keep the heat build-up to a minimum. A pink or white wheel would produce a similar grind, but the heat will build quicker, necessitating shorter grinding sessions between periods of cooling.

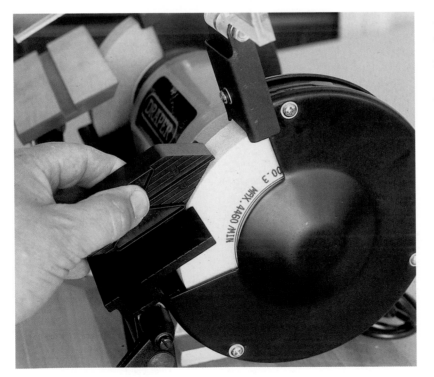

2 Use a template or gauge to set the angle of the table in respect of the wheel. In this case, the primary grind is to be 25°.

3 Set the plane iron square into the grinding jig, ensuring that the iron just contacts the wheel.

4 Start the grinder and move the iron from side to side across the wheel, applying light pressure, until the bevel has been formed. The iron is now ready for finer honing and polishing by hand.

3:5 Turning tools

Turning tools are very different from the chisels and plane irons discussed so far. The cutting action is powered (the operator presents the tool to the work while a lathe provides the turning action) the forces bearing down on the cutting edge are far in excess of those put on bench tools, and the angle of attack much steeper.

For these reasons, turning tools are on the whole more robust than bench tools – even the small tools used on miniature lathes for making pens, lace bobbins and so on are, by necessity, stout in their structure.

Cabinetmakers have their own preferences for the sharpening of their tools, but are, on the whole, fairly limited as to what they can change. A few degrees of bevel change either side of 30° is about it.

Turners on the other hand have an entire armoury of gouges, chisels, scrapers, parting tools, as well as a mass of specialist tools like beaders, thread chasers and so on. All these tools require different methods of sharpening, but there is a huge range of accessories available to make the turner's life easier.

It is beyond the scope of this book to discuss the various types of sharpening accessory available to woodturners and how to use them – it would be too easy for this section to become a catalogue of what is available. For the most part, the instructions supplied with the sharpening jigs and other equipment are more than adequate for the task. There would be little benefit in having a translated version reproduced here.

Grinding turning tools

The number-one rule with dry grinding, especially with turning tools, is to use eye protection. Sparks and debris are showered over the operator during the sharpening process, and it is vital to have protection. Also, make sure that there are no flammables, liquid or solid, within range of the sparks – which includes rags and wire wool.

ABOVE A selection of turning tools.

Although it is perfectly possible to sharpen turning tools on a conventional grinder, a slow-speed grinder offers more control and reduces the risk of overheating the tool. Such grinders are usually fitted with white wheels and run at approximately half the speed of a conventional machine. The model shown in the following step-by-step sequence (overleaf) is fitted with 40mm wide aluminium-oxide wheels: one coarse wheel (60 grit) for profiling and grinding out nicks and damage, and a fine wheel (100 grit) for sharpening.

These grinders are fitted with better tool rests than some cheaper models, but can still benefit from the fitting of new tool rests and accessories.

Slow-speed grinders were originally developed for sharpening turning tools, but can also be used to grind bench tools (and they are particularly useful when grinding fine-bladed tools). The slower speed means that metal is removed from the edge at a slower rate. This will make the grinding easier to control, but it will obviously also take more time.

(FOCUS ON:

Grinding Angles

For the roughing gouge used in the step-by-step instructions in this chapter (see page 152), the conventional wisdom is to grind the bevel to 45°. However, some turners prefer a lesser angle. There are no hard-and-fast rules, just starting points, and this is something the novice may find strange. In order to find out what suits your particular needs you will need to experiment. Start with 45° grind and try it. Then reduce the angle of grind and try again. Compare the results and keep experimenting until you have a grind you are happy with.

LEFT Start with a 45° grind for the primary bevel of a roughing gouge such as this.

(FOCUS ON:

Grinding Angles

Setting up a turner's half-speed dry grinder

1 This Creusen half-speed dry grinder is supplied, as standard, with small but very solid adjustable tool rests. Creusen also make specialist attachments for this grinder, but they are for specific tasks such as grinding straight-edged tools or sharpening drill bits.

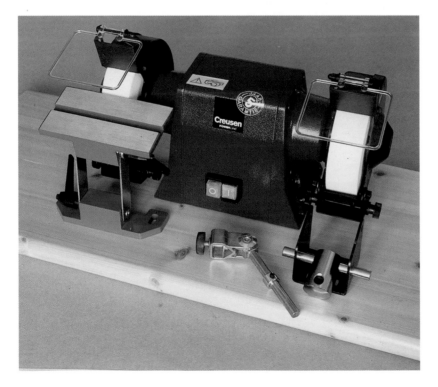

2 This machine is to be mounted on a grinder stand along with a Fingernail Profiler and a larger tool rest. Each side of the machine's mounting board is drilled so that the jigs can be used on either wheel.

3 Alternatively, the tool rests supplied with the grinder can be swung back into position.

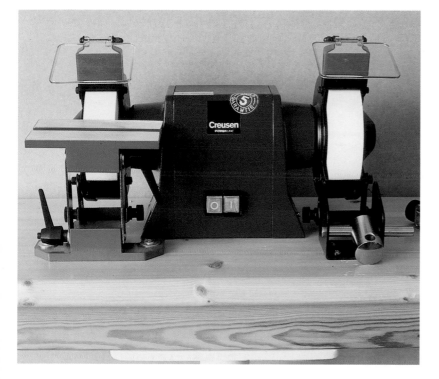

4 All set up and ready for work. The block under the mounting board raises the grinder to a more comfortable height (for me) to work at.

Grinding turning tools – some basics

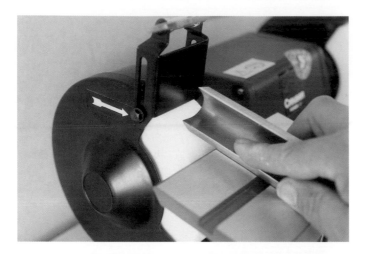

1 With the grinder stationary, set the tool rest to the preferred sharpening angle. This is conventionally 45° for the roughing gouge used in this example.

2 Using one hand, hold the tool flat on the tool rest, in line with the wheel, and hold the handle with the other. Move the tool up to the wheel and gently rotate while applying light pressure. Take your time and do not try to force the procedure by applying more pressure. Keep the tool moving and do not let it stop in one place, otherwise a 'flat' will be made in the bevel, spoiling the smooth shape.

3 If this is the first grind and you are establishing the shape, you may find a burr in the inside of the gouge – this should be honed with a slip stone.

4 Whilst turning a piece, frequent retouching may be necessary to keep the performance of the tool constant; doing this freehand will save time. Present the tool so that the heel of the bevel is in line with the wheel, and then bring it down until contact is made. At this point, rotate the tool to sharpen it. This will not give as good an edge as using a tool rest, but it will keep you turning.

5 Spindle gouges are notoriously hard to sharpen without a jig, although, with practice, not impossible. The tool needs to be swung from side to side through a constant arc while it is being rotated in order to grind the whole of the bevel.

6 A fingernail jig makes this easy. The jig can be set to accommodate a wide range of profiles and sizes.

Grinding turning tools – some basics

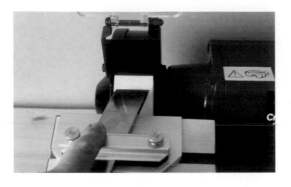

7 Chisels and skew chisels are ground on the tool rest. A clamp-style guide can be used for initial grinding. The angle can be drawn onto the rest as a guide for touching up.

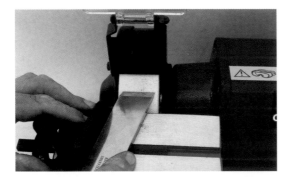

8 The mitre gauge is also useful for touching up skew chisels at a specified angle.

9 After grinding, a chisel should be honed to a finer finish. This is easier to do with the chisel held firm and a stone passed over the edge. A good-size bench stone is the preferred tool here – slip stones are just too small for this work.

10 Scrapers are honed to a mirror finish on the face using a bench stone in much the same way as a plane iron is flattened. As with the plane iron this is only necessary when new, so it is worth spending the time getting the best finish you can along its whole length.

11 Regardless of shape, a scraper should be ground to an angle of around 70°. The intention is to grind the scraper just enough to leave a slight burr on the top edge. It is this burr that will do the cutting. Judging this burr just right on a grinder is something of an art. Not enough and the burr will be too fine, too much and it will curl over away from the wood and not cut.

12 Alternatively, the scraper can be ground to a 45° angle and the top edge can be honed back to 70° using a bench stone. A medium-grit ceramic stone is good for this as it can be used dry and will not wear the stone unduly. The resultant burr is left intact and should cut well.

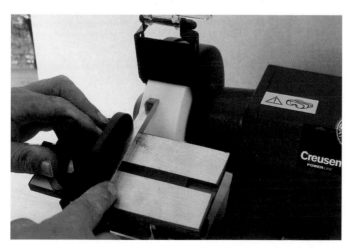

13 Parting tools are treated like chisels, but care needs to be taken to keep the grind square to the edge of the tool.

3:6 Carving tools

From the roughing out down to the finest of details, the quality of your carving depends on using tools with a good edge. This demand for a high-quality finish combined with the huge variety of profiles available means that, although the basics still apply, the methods used to sharpen carving tools are extensive – as is the range of equipment.

However, the tools themselves are usually lovingly produced to a very high standard, and new ones will probably only require a final polish. Where this is the case, grinding will only be necessary if the edge sustains damage or the profile of the tool needs to be altered.

The key to keeping carving tools in good working order is continuous polishing – your aim should be to keep the tool permanently sharp using a strop. In practice, the edge eventually becomes rounded and the cutting efficiency drops. The length of time this will take to correct depends on the skill of the sharpener and the rigidity of the honing medium.

Waterstones of varying grit have been used in the following step-by-step sequences, but oil, ceramic or diamond stones would be equally effective.

Honing and stropping carving tools

1 A profiled waterstone and slip stone are soaked for 10 minutes before use.

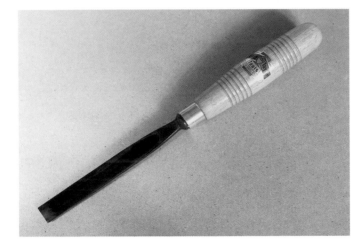

2 This Henry Taylor straight gouge is supplied beautifully ground and ready to have the final edge honed to perfection (or as near as possible).

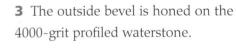

3 The outside bevel is honed on the 4000-grit profiled waterstone.

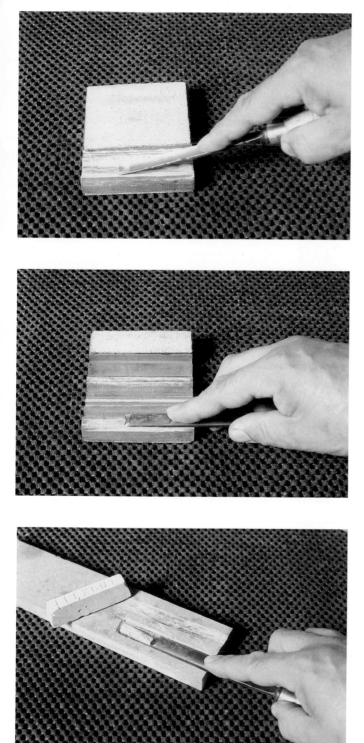

4 It is then polished on a Flexcut profiled strop, which has been charged with polishing compound.

5 Remove the burr by honing the inside of the profile on the convex portions of the strop.

6 Alternatively, a custom-made strop can be created by carving the profiles, both concave and convex, into a piece of MDF. The profiles are charged with compound in the same way as the Flexcut strop, and used in the same manner. Bespoke strops like this are useful for your favourite gouges. Kept close at hand while carving they make it easy to keep the edge crisp.

Honing and stropping carving tools

7 Small nicks and the like can be ground out using coarser stones. This 1000-grit conical stone is being used to regrind the bevel after a small nick appeared.

8 Once the bevel has been reformed, a 4000-grit stone is used to finish the bevel prior to stropping.

9 Small gouges can be sharpened on a profiled stone. Continued use will 'mould' the stone to the gouge.

10 The inside can be de-burred with a fine teardrop profiled slip stone.

11 V-shaped tools need to be treated as two matched flat tools as far as initial honing of the bevel is concerned. An equal amount of material should be removed from each side – e.g. five strokes on one bevel needs to be balanced with five strokes on the other.

12 The point of the 'V' is rounded slightly after honing to prevent the tool from being dragged deeper into the wood by the cutting action and creating tearout.

13 The inner faces are honed on a strop or slip stone with a sharp profile. Make sure the pressure is applied to the back of the bevel and not the corner where the faces meet.

Honing and stropping carving tools

14 Straight chisels can be honed on bench stones or the back of the profiled stone or even the flat side of a slip stone.

15 Curved gouges are honed in the same way as straight gouges. However, I find that the shape of them makes them awkward to hone and strop by hand. Power honing is the answer.

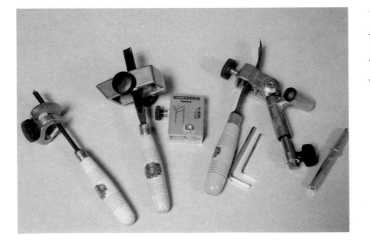

16 The Tormek system works extremely well for carving tools. By using the appropriate honing jig, a repeatable grind can be produced.

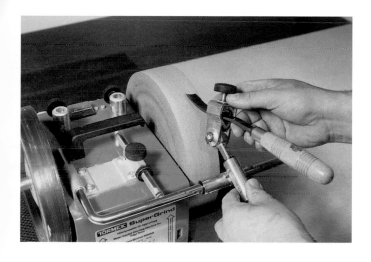

17 The fine grinding wheel will produce a superb finish, which can be honed to a mirror finish on the flat or profiled leather honing wheels.

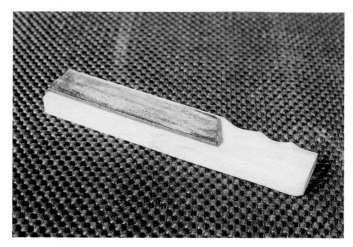

18 Stropping is how the edge is maintained on a day-to-day basis. The first thing to do is to make a strop. This is a piece of wood with a handle fashioned at one end and a length of leather glued to it, rough side up. These can be custom made in the workshop using an old leather belt as the source of the leather, or can be purchased ready made from some suppliers.

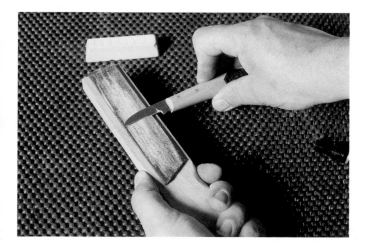

19 The leather is charged with stropping compound and the blade is worked away from the edge to produce the ultimate sharpness.

Sharpening chip carving knives

1 Chip carving knives are best sharpened by hand. This typical collection of knives is supplied ready-ground and set for final honing and stropping. This is probably one of the simplest looking of all sharpening jobs – but looks can be deceptive.

2 The hardest thing to do is to maintain that perfectly flat bevel. Any slight rocking of the wrist will produce a curved, convex bevel. On such a small surface this will dramatically change the cutting angle.

3 Practise getting the technique right using a block of hard wood and a felt-tip pen. Colour the bevel of the knife and 'hone' the knife on the wood.

4 To find the correct angle at which to hone, rest the knife flat on the wooden block and lightly progress forward until the edge begins to remove the finest of dust from the surface of the wood. This is about the angle you need to be.

5 Continue to 'hone' the edge on the wood, inspecting it regularly to see where the ink is being removed. The aim is to remove the ink evenly across the bevel.

6 Although the mild abrasive qualities of the wood will polish the bevel slightly, no significant amount of material will be removed. Once the correct 'feel' has been established, the technique can be used on a fine stone. Use the pen to mark the edge and make a couple of light passes. The ink should have been totally removed, confirming a flat honing technique.

Converting a cheap grinder into a power strop

1 This cheap grinder can easily be converted into a power strop. The problem is that a grinder runs with the top of the wheel turning towards you. In order to strop the edge of a tool the wheel needs to run in the opposite direction.

2 All that needs to be done is to remove the guards and replace them on the opposite ends. This effectively makes the back the front, and the wheels will now rotate away from you.

3 Replace the grinding wheels with felt wheels and you have an inexpensive, reverse-running power strop. The only problem is the on-off switch is on the back. However, this could be remedied if found to be a major inconvenience.

ABOVE The addition of a larger tool rest and different wheels at each end further enhance the flexibility of this machine.

Conclusion

Now you know how to create a good edge, the knife that you use to carve the Sunday roast will be in for a shock. After applying some of your newly found skills, you will be able to produce wafer-thin slices of beef and dissect over-ripe tomatoes without squashing them.

Use those coarse, grey grinding wheels in the grinder to sharpen rotary mower blades, and other less subtle garden tools. Edged tools will need a bit more finesse, but now you should have the basic skills to produce an edge on most domestic equipment, as well as your own personal woodworking tools.

If you have read this far into this book you are probably thinking that you have gained a good knowledge of sharpening, and, hopefully, you have a solid foundation on which to build. However, it is now that the real learning curve begins. There is no substitute for experience. Watch a professional woodturner touch up his tools and it will seem to require no more thought or effort than breathing – that is a sign of experience.

Glossary

A

Abrasive

Technically, any material that can be used to abrade another. In processes that grind, lap or hone, abrasives are typically limited to hard natural and synthetic substances, the most common minerals being crystalline forms of aluminium oxide, silicon carbide and diamond. Stropping and polishing can be carried out on much softer materials, such as leather and newspaper.

Abrasive Grains

Individual grits of abrasive mineral; also called grit.

Aluminium Oxide

A long-life grit commonly used for bench stones, grinding wheels and abrasive papers. Aluminium oxide is in fact a synthetic form of the natural mineral 'corundum' and is produced synthetically by refining bauxite ore. There are many variations in products and the related trade names often arise from differences in manufacturing processes. Some modern versions are sintered to produce an extremely fine crystalline structure. (See Superabrasives).

Arc of Contact

The small portion of a grinding wheel where abrasive grains actually contact with the tool edge. This is the region where heat is generated during grinding.

B

Bench Stone

Also known as a whetstone. A stone used for sharpening edged tools. The main types are waterstones, oilstones, diamond stones and ceramic stones.

Bond

The material used to hold the abrasive grains (or grit) in place in bench stones and grinding wheels. Bonding materials can be resins, epoxy, rubber, metal and vitrified materials, and the strength of the bond determines the 'hardness' of the stone/wheel. In the early days of grinding-wheel production the proportions of abrasive and binder were rather hit and miss. Today, the formulae are closely guarded and vary from one manufacturer to another.

Burning

Physical changes to a tool edge caused by overheating during the grinding process. Burning is usually associated with changes in metallurgical properties and can be seen as a discoloration of the edge. The effected area should be ground away, as it will no longer be possible to maintain a sharp edge.

Burr

An undesirable ragged metal ridge that is created as an edge is sharpened. This should be removed by passing the back up and down a fine stone a couple of times, holding it perfectly flat on the surface.

C

Carborundum

Trade name. Carborundum is silicone-carbide abrasive mineral that was especially common during the DIY revolution of the 1950s, and is still in widespread use today.

CBN

An abbreviation for cubic Boron Nitride. CBN is a superabrasive with a hardness second only to diamond. Like diamond, it is produced through a high-temperature, high-pressure process that makes it more expensive than conventional abrasives.

Corundum

A natural mineral principally composed of aluminium oxide. Historically a mineral mined in the Middle East and India, it has now been replaced by synthetic abrasive minerals, which offer more uniform and consistent physical properties.

D

Diamond

A natural and synthetic mineral composed of carbon atoms in a specific crystalline structure. Industrial diamonds can be used to produce tools for dressing grinding wheels. Synthetic diamond is manufactured in a special high-temperature, high-pressure process and subsequently treated to make a variety of abrasive grains.

Dressing

A process to expose fresh abrasive on a grinding wheel, usually using a diamond-based abrasive tool. Dressing removes glazed material and worn abrasive grains to restore the grinding-wheel surface for more efficient material removal and to prevent burning. It can also be used to restore the shape of (i.e. flatten) contoured surfaces. Not to be confused with truing.

G

Glazing

A characteristic of conventional abrasive surfaces. If the bond fails to release abrasive grains properly during use, the surface becomes clogged (i.e. glazed). Glazed wheels have a polished surface appearance and the resultant loss of cutting efficiency can lead to edge overheating.

Grade

A term used to indicate the relative hardness of a grinding-wheel bond structure. The degree of hardness is indicated by a code letter ranging from A to Z. It is unusual for a wheel grade to be much lower (i.e. softer) than D or E, while a Z classification would indicate a very hard bond indeed. You could have a stock of various grades of wheel to suit different tasks, but an I or J will suffice as a general-purpose abrasive.

Grinding

The removal of metal from a tool using an abrasive product. The primary bevel on general-purpose woodworking tools such as chisels and plane irons are frequently set (or altered) using a high-speed dry grinder, although bench stones can also be used.

Grit

The abrasive particles used to make conventional abrasive products. Grit size is traditionally based on mesh sizes, where the number indicates openings per inch of screening mesh. However, a number of other measurement systems are also common – for example, measurements for very small grit size in units of millionths of a metre (or microns). Most grinding wheels fit into a medium band of 60 to 120 grit, while abrasive papers can be as fine as 2000 grit.

H

Heat Treatment

Altering the properties of a metal by subjecting it to a sequence of temperature changes (also known as tempering). The time of retention at specific temperature (soaking) and rate of cooling (quenching) are as important as the temperature itself. Heat treatment affects properties such as strength, hardness, ductility and malleability.

Honing

Historically, a term meaning to achieve a fine finish, but now used as a general name for sharpening and polishing.

L

Lapping

A hand-sharpening process using loose abrasive grains and a fluid. It is also a useful technique for flattening bench stones.

P

Polishing

A process producing a very fine finish to a sharp edge and involving little or no material removal (in contrast to grinding).

Q

Quenching

Cooling the edge during sharpening to prevent overheating. Quenching is especially important when using a high-speed dry grinder and when grinding small, delicate tools.

R

Resin Bond

A common type of bond formed from a synthetic resin that can be cured by thermal, ultraviolet light or other methods. Resin bonds are typically identified in the standard wheel marking by the letter B, derived from Bakelite, one of the first resin-bond materials.

Rubber Bond

A bond of synthetic or natural rubber used for grinding wheels and identified by the letter R in standard wheel markings.

S

Sandpaper

A traditional form of coated abrasive paper. The name refers to early forms that used sand glued to paper.

Silicon Carbide

A synthetic mineral commonly used as a conventional abrasive in grinding wheels. Silicon carbide fractures more easily and is harder than aluminium oxide, and is typically used in applications where its sharper cutting characteristics are an advantage.

Strop

An abrasive strip, most commonly wood or leather, used in combination with a polishing compound to produce a very fine finish to a sharp edge.

Superabrasives

A new generation of sophisticated abrasive materials, usually CBN (cubic Boron Nitride) or industrial diamond. While superabrasives offer 'super' performance and are very hard wearing, the more conventional forms of abrasive (especially the latest microcrystalline sintered grinding wheels) are more than adequate when it comes to sharpening woodworking tools.

T

Truing

A process to correct the concentricity and shape of a grinding wheel. Truing is designed to reduce vibration and produce a uniform cutting rate. This process should not be confused with dressing, which removes glazed bond material to expose fresh abrasive grains.

V

Vitrified bond

A relatively common bond manufactured from fusible powdered glasses along with fillers such as graphite or copper. These bonds are harder than metal bonds, but not as strong. As a result, they produce less friction and have a freer cutting action. Vitrified bonds are mostly used for precise, lower-speed operations.

W

Wet-and-dry paper

A type of fine abrasive paper that can be used with lubrication, either water or mineral spirits. The grit is generally of silicon carbide and the paper and glue are waterproof.

About the Author

Ralph Laughton originally trained as an engineer, but did not follow that path. Instead, on leaving full-time education he embarked on a career as an editor for a specialist publisher. This led him into the world of graphic design, where he found it possible to indulge a creative passion for well over twenty years. It was at this point that he decided to take an opportunity to realize a life-long dream. Ralph is now a full-time woodworker, designing and building furniture, repairing old joinery and writing about the techniques that he has spent nearly forty years acquiring. He is a resident expert for *New Woodworking* magazine and also writes a regular column in *The Router*, both published by the Guild of Master Craftsman.

Index

Titles available from

GMC Publications

Books

Woodcarving

Beginning Woodcarving	GMC Publications
Carving Architectural Detail in Wood:	
The Classical Tradition	Frederick Wilbur
Carving Birds & Beasts	GMC Publications
Carving Classical Styles in Wood	Frederick Wilbur
Carving the Human Figure: Studies in Wood and Stone	Dick Onians
Carving Nature: Wildlife Studies in Wood	Frank Fox-Wilson
Celtic Carved Lovespoons: 30 Patterns	Sharon Littley & Clive Griffin
Decorative Woodcarving (New Edition)	Jeremy Williams
Elements of Woodcarving	Chris Pye
Figure Carving in Wood: Human and Animal Forms	Sara Wilkinson
Lettercarving in Wood: A Practical Course	Chris Pye
Relief Carving in Wood: A Practical Introduction	Chris Pye
Woodcarving for Beginners	GMC Publications
Woodcarving Made Easy	Cynthia Rogers
Woodcarving Tools, Materials & Equipment (New Edition in 2 vols.) Chris Pye	

Woodturning

Bowl Turning Techniques Masterclass	Tony Boase
Chris Child's Projects for Woodturners	Chris Child
Decorating Turned Wood: The Maker's Eye	Liz & Michael O'Donnell
Green Woodwork	Mike Abbott
A Guide to Work-Holding on the Lathe	Fred Holder
Keith Rowley's Woodturning Projects	Keith Rowley
Making Screw Threads in Wood	Fred Holder
Segmented Turning: A Complete Guide	Ron Hampton
Turned Boxes: 50 Designs	Chris Stott
Turning Green Wood	Michael O'Donnell
Turning Pens and Pencils	Kip Christensen & Rex Burningham
Wood for Woodturners	Mark Baker
Woodturning: Forms and Materials	John Hunnex
Woodturning: A Foundation Course (New Edition)	Keith Rowley
Woodturning: A Fresh Approach	Robert Chapman
Woodturning: An Individual Approach	Dave Regester
Woodturning: A Source Book of Shapes	John Hunnex
Woodturning Masterclass	Tony Boase
Woodturning Projects: A Workshop Guide to Shapes	Mark Baker

Woodworking

Beginning Picture Marquetry	Lawrence Threadgold
Carcass Furniture	GMC Publications
Celtic Carved Lovespoons: 30 Patterns	Sharon Littley & Clive Griffin
Celtic Woodcraft	Glenda Bennett
Celtic Woodworking Projects	Glenda Bennett
Complete Woodfinishing (Revised Edition)	Ian Hosker
David Charlesworth's Furniture-Making Techniques	David Charlesworth
David Charlesworth's Furniture-Making Techniques –	
Volume 2	David Charlesworth
Furniture Projects with the Router	Kevin Ley
Furniture Restoration (Practical Crafts)	Kevin Jan Bonner
Furniture Restoration: A Professional at Work	John Lloyd
Furniture Workshop	Kevin Ley

Green Woodwork	Mike Abbott
History of Furniture: Ancient to 1900	Michael Huntley
Intarsia: 30 Patterns for the Scrollsaw	John Everett
Making Heirloom Boxes	Peter Lloyd
Making Screw Threads in Wood	Fred Holder
Making Woodwork Aids and Devices	Robert Wearing
Mastering the Router	Ron Fox
Pine Furniture Projects for the Home	Dave Mackenzie
Router Magic: Jigs, Fixtures and Tricks to	
Unleash your Router's Full Potential	Bill Hylton
Router Projects for the Home	GMC Publications
Router Tips & Techniques	Robert Wearing
Routing: A Workshop Handbook	Anthony Bailey
Routing for Beginners (Revised and Expanded Edition)	Anthony Bailey
Stickmaking: A Complete Course	Andrew Jones & Clive George
Stickmaking Handbook	Andrew Jones & Clive George
Storage Projects for the Router	GMC Publications
Veneering: A Complete Course	Ian Hosker
Veneering Handbook	Ian Hosker
Wood: Identification & Use	Terry Porter
Woodworking Techniques and Projects	Anthony Bailey
Woodworking with the Router: Professional	
Router Techniques any Woodworker can Use	Bill Hylton & Fred Matlack

Upholstery

Upholstery: A Beginners' Guide	David James
Upholstery: A Complete Course (Revised Edition)	David James
Upholstery Restoration	David James
Upholstery Techniques & Projects	David James
Upholstery Tips and Hints	David James

Dolls' Houses and Miniatures

1/12 Scale Character Figures for the Dolls' House	James Carrington
Americana in 1/12 Scale:	
50 Authentic Projects	Joanne Ogreenc & Mary Lou Santovec
The Authentic Georgian Dolls' House	Brian Long
A Beginners' Guide to the Dolls' House Hobby	Jean Nisbett
Celtic, Medieval and Tudor Wall Hangings in	
1/12 Scale Needlepoint	Sandra Whitehead
Creating Decorative Fabrics: Projects in 1/12 Scale	Janet Storey
Dolls' House Accessories, Fixtures and Fittings	Andrea Barham
Dolls' House Furniture: Easy-to-Make Projects in 1/12 Scale	Freida Gray
Dolls' House Makeovers	Jean Nisbett
Dolls' House Window Treatments	Eve Harwood
Edwardian-Style Hand-Knitted Fashion	
for 1/12 Scale Dolls	Yvonne Wakefield
How to Make Your Dolls' House Special:	
Fresh Ideas for Decorating	Beryl Armstrong
Making 1/12 Scale Wicker Furniture for the Dolls' House	Sheila Smith
Making Miniature Chinese Rugs and Carpets	Carol Phillipson
Making Miniature Food and Market Stalls	Angie Scarr
Making Miniature Gardens	Freida Gray
Making Miniature Oriental Rugs & Carpets	Meik & Ian McNaughton
Making Miniatures: Projects for the	
1/12 Scale Dolls' House	Christiane Berridge
Making Period Dolls' House Accessories	Andrea Barham

Magazines

WOODTURNING ◆ WOODCARVING ◆ FURNITURE & CABINETMAKING ◆ THE ROUTER
NEW WOODWORKING ◆ THE DOLLS' HOUSE MAGAZINE ◆ OUTDOOR PHOTOGRAPHY
BLACK & WHITE PHOTOGRAPHY ◆ KNITTING
GUILD NEWS

The above represents a full list of all titles currently published or scheduled to be published.
All are available direct from the Publishers or through bookshops, newsagents and specialist retailers.
To place an order, or to obtain a complete catalogue, contact:

GMC Publications

Castle Place, 166 High Street, Lewes, East Sussex BN7 1XU, United Kingdom
Tel: 01273 488005 Fax: 01273 402866
E-mail: pubs@thegmcgroup.com Website: www.gmcbooks.com

ORDERS BY CREDIT CARD ARE ACCEPTED